From Your Friends At The MAILBOX®

23 Ready-To-Go Lesson Plans

SOCIAL STUDIES

GRADE 1

www.themailbox.com

What Are Lifesaver Lessons®?

Lifesaver Lessons® are well-planned, easy-to-implement, curriculum-based lessons. Each lesson contains a complete materials list, step-by-step instructions, a reproducible activity or pattern, and several extension activities.

How Do I Use A Lifesaver Lessons® Unit?

Each Lifesaver Lesson is designed to decrease your preparation time and increase the amount of quality teaching time with your students. These lessons are great for introducing or reinforcing new concepts. Use the handy list below to see what types of materials to gather. After completing a lesson, be sure to check out the fun-filled extension activities.

What Materials Will I Need?

Most of the materials for each lesson can be easily found in your classroom or school. Check the list of materials below for any items you may need to gather or purchase.

- crayons
- construction paper
- markers
- pins
- drawing paper
- scissors
- glue
- chart paper
- any two children's books that you have not read to your class
- stapler
- globe
- small container
- game markers
- duplicating paper
- yarn
- hole puncher
- grocery bag
- stapler

Project Editor:
Sharon Murphy

Writers:
Darcy Brown, Rebecca Brudwick, Lisa Buchholz, Stacie Stone Davis, Jill Hamilton, Lisa Kelly, Geoff Mihalenko, Laura A. Mihalenko, Sandy Shaw

Artists:
Cathy Spangler Bruce, Pam Crane, Teresa R. Davidson, Nick Greenwood, Sheila Krill, Theresa Lewis, Rob Mayworth, Kimberly Richard, Barry Slate, Donna K. Teal

Cover Artist:
Kimberly Richard

Table Of Contents

Me & My Community

Self-Esteem 3
Different Family Structures 7
Community Helpers 11

Government & Citizenship

Rules At Home And School 15
Classroom Citizenship 19
Classroom Rights And Responsibilities 23
Democratic Decision Making 27
United States Symbols 31

Map Skills

Map Symbols And Map Keys 35
Creating A Classroom Map 39
Cardinal Directions 43

Our Neighbors

Holidays Around The World 47
Families Around The World 51
Homes Around The World 55

History

Sequencing Holidays On A Timeline 59
Schools Of Today And The Past 63
Significant Historical Figures 67

Economics

Needs And Wants 71
Shortages 75
Goods And Services 79
Producers And Consumers 83
Money As A Means Of Exchange 87
Division Of Labor 91

Answer Keys 95

Management Checklist 96

www.themailbox.com

ISBN #1-56234-305-X

Manufactured in the United States
10 9 8 7 6 5 4 3 2 1

Superhero Students

It's a bird! It's a plane! No, it's a classroom of super students! Use this high-interest activity to help your students' self-esteem grow by leaps and bounds!

Skill: Identifying and describing one's strengths and accomplishments

Estimated Lesson Time: 40 minutes

Teacher Preparation:

1. Duplicate page 5 for each student.
2. Duplicate the badge pattern shown below for each student.
3. Cut a large badge from red paper. Label the paper with a large *S*. Pin the paper to your shirt.

Materials:

1 copy of page 5 per student
1 badge pattern per student
red paper
black marker
1 pin per student (plus one extra)
crayons

S

I am a
SUPER STUDENT
because ____________
____
____
____

Introducing The Lesson:

Show students the large badge on your shirt. Explain to students that you are Super Teacher. Ask students to imagine what powers you might have. After several responses, reveal to students a unique quality or talent you have or a recent accomplishment.

Steps:

1. Ask students to think about their favorite superheroes. Have students describe some characteristics of well-known superheroes. Ask students to include internal as well as external qualities. Then tell students that superheroes are unique because of these qualities they possess.

2. Ask students to think of talents or qualities they have that make them super. Write students' responses on the chalkboard. Then give each child a badge pattern and direct him to complete the sentence. Encourage students to include in the sentence a special quality or talent that he thinks makes him special. Pin each child's badge to his shirt.

3. Distribute a copy of page 5 to each student. Read each sentence aloud and provide time for students to complete it. Provide help as needed. Then have each child draw a face and hair on the superhero figure to resemble himself.

4. Invite students to share their completed work with their classmates.

Name ______________________________

Superhero Students

Congratulations! You are a superhero student.
Complete the sentences.
Draw your face.

1. Something special I can do is ______________________________
______________________________.
2. I know a lot about ______________________________
______________________________.
3. At school I'm good at ______________________________
______________________________.
4. At home I'm good at ______________________________
______________________________.
5. I'm proud that I ______________________________
______________________________.
6. My favorite thing about me is ______________________________
______________________________.

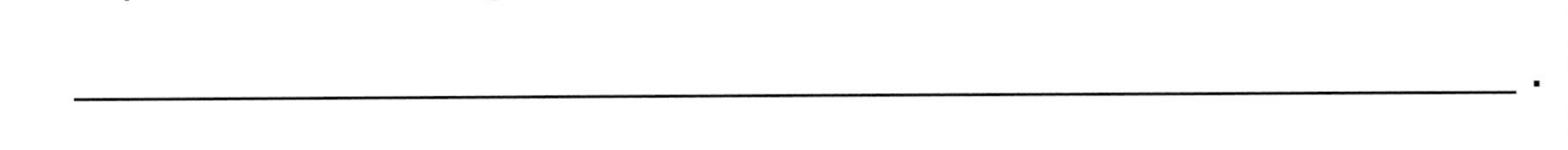

How To Extend The Lesson:

- Cereal boxes often feature heroes. With this kid-tested, teacher-approved activity, each student makes himself the star of a cereal box. Ask each child to bring an empty cereal box to school. Then give each student a white sheet of construction paper that is the same size as the front panel of the box. The student positions the paper vertically and draws a picture of himself and his special talent. Then he titles his cereal box and writes a sentence describing the picture. Finally he glues the paper to the front of the cereal box. Display the completed projects for students to see just how special everyone is!

- Acknowledge students' special accomplishments with this ongoing display. Cut out a supply of hand shapes from colorful paper and place them in an easily accessible location. Each time a student meets a goal or accomplishes a special feat, write his name and a description of the task on a hand cutout. Then mount the cutouts on a display titled "High Five For Super Students!"

- Create a class book featuring a page of compliments for each student. Purchase or make a journal, and label a page for each student. Add construction-paper stars to the cover along with a title, such as "[Teacher's name]'s Shining Stars." Place the journal and a pencil in an easily accessible location. Encourage students to write compliments about their classmates on the corresponding pages. No doubt students will enjoy reading this book time and time again!

- Build self-esteem with mirrors that help your students see themselves in a positive light. Look into a handheld mirror and say several positive statements about yourself. Then discuss with students what *self-acceptance* means. Next give each student a mirror-shaped cutout similar to the one shown. In the middle of the mirror, instruct each student to draw a picture of herself. Then have her decorate the mirror and write several self-descriptive words around the portrait. What a great way for students to see their true reflections!

Fantastic Families

Fathers, mothers, sisters, brothers!
Families are great because they love each other!

Skill: Recognizing different family structures

Estimated Lesson Time: 45 minutes

Teacher Preparation:
Duplicate page 9 for each student.

Materials:
1 copy of page 9 per student
1 sheet of drawing paper per student
crayons

Background Information:
There are many different kinds of families.

- *nuclear family:* a mother, father, and their children living together in a family
- *blended family* or *stepfamily:* when parents from different nuclear families live together with their children in a family
- *extended family:* when relatives live together in a family
- *single-parent family:* when only one parent lives with a family
- *foster family:* a family taking care of a child they did not give birth to for a limited period of time
- *adoptive family:* when parents have a child that they did not give birth to

Introducing The Lesson:

Give each child a sheet of drawing paper and have her quickly draw a picture of her family. After students complete their drawings, invite student volunteers to share their pictures.

Steps:

1. Explain to students that not all families are the same. For example, some families have more members than others. Some families include parents and grandparents living in the same house. And some families have only one parent living in the house. Use the Background Information on page 7 as you discuss with students different types of families. Then tell students that although families are different they have some things in common: all families care about each other and share their lives together.

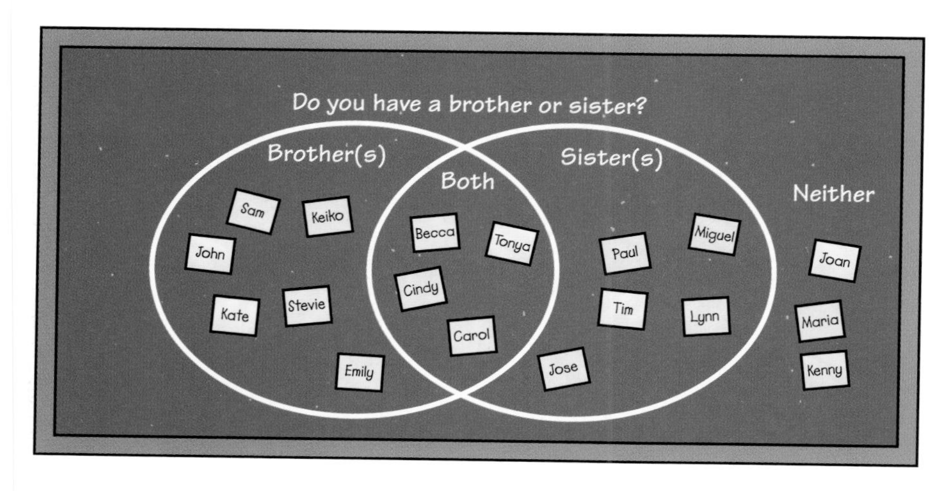

2. Next use a Venn diagram to help students learn about their classmates' families. To do this, label a Venn diagram like the one shown. Have each student write her name on a sticky note and, in turn, attach the note to the appropriate area of the diagram. When all of the data has been collected, lead students in evaluating the diagram.

3. Distribute a copy of page 9 to each student. Explain to students that the goal of the activity is to collect a signature in each box. Remind students that they may only sign true facts about themselves, and they may only sign each reproducible one time. Set a time limit of approximately 10 to 15 minutes; then have students begin the activity.

4. Announce when time is up and have students return to their desks. In turn, read aloud each statement on the grid and invite students to share the names of classmates who signed that box.

5. Challenge students to complete the Bonus Box activity.

Name ____________________ *Recognizing different family structures*

Fantastic Families

Follow your teacher's directions.

Is the youngest in the family	Has a stepfamily	Is an only child
Has more than one brother or sister	Has a grandparent	Has an older brother or sister
Has a younger brother or sister	Has a cousin he or she likes to play with	Has an aunt or uncle

Bonus Box: Put a ✓ in each box that describes your family.

How To Extend The Lesson:

- Share the following family-friendly literature with your youngsters.
  - — *Who's Who In My Family* by Loreen Leedy (Holiday House, Inc.; 1995)
  - — *Fathers, Mothers, Sisters, Brothers: A Collection Of Family Poems* by Mary Ann Hoberman (Puffin Books, 1993)
  - — *Celebrating Families* by Rosmarie Hausherr (Scholastic Inc., 1997)

- These family pennants are the perfect way for students to show how wonderful their families are! On a large pennant cutout, a student draws lines dividing the pennant into three sections. Next she draws what her family does for fun in the first section. On the middle section, she illustrates her family working together. In the remaining section, she draws her family showing love to one another. Mount the pennants on a bulletin board titled "Three Cheers For Family!"

- Students see the variety of family structures with this nifty idea. Each student will need access to Unifix® cubes in eight different colors. Post a chart like the one shown. Read aloud the first step and provide time for students to gather a green cube. Continue in this same manner for the remaining steps, as students connect additional cubes to create a personalized tower. Encourage students to include stepfamilies and half-siblings in their towers. Then invite each child to share her resulting tower and challenge her classmates to evaluate it. What a fun and colorful way to learn about families!

Discovering Community Helpers

The result of this fun-filled activity is a class book describing a variety of community helpers.

Skill: Identifying the roles of community helpers

Estimated Lesson Time: 45 minutes

Teacher Preparation:
Duplicate page 13 for each student.

Materials:
1 copy of page 13 per student
crayons

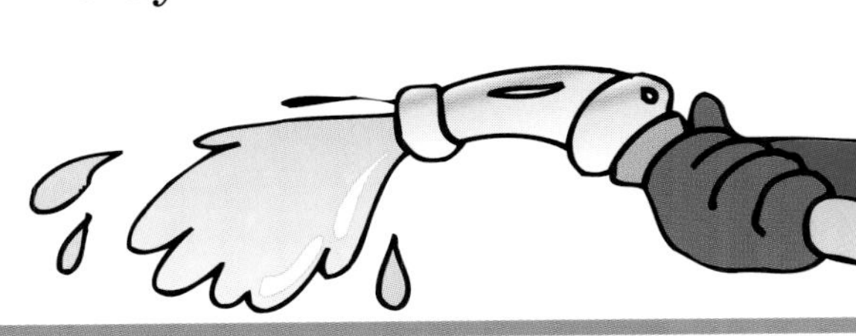

Background Information:
Community helpers include the following:

actor
architect
artist
astronaut
baker
banker
bus driver
carpenter
chef
coach
construction worker
dentist
doctor
farmer
firefighter
flight attendant
florist
garbage collector
hairstylist
janitor
lawyer
librarian
mail carrier
mechanic
meteorologist
musician
news reporter
nurse
pharmacist
photographer
pilot
plumber
police officer
principal
scientist
seamstress
teacher
travel agent
truck driver
veterinarian
waitperson
writer

Introducing The Lesson:

Read the following clues about a firefighter to your students: "I ride in a big red truck. I wear special clothes to protect myself from fires. I use a long hose to put out fires. Who am I?" Call on a volunteer to give the answer. Then tell students that they are going to play a game called Who Am I? to help them learn the roles of several community helpers.

Steps:

1. Ask a student volunteer to come to the front of the classroom. Whisper the name of a community helper in his ear (refer to page 11 for a list of community helpers). Next have the student give clues to his classmates that describe the community helper. Remind the student to end his set of clues by saying, "Who am I?" Then have his classmates guess the identity of the community helper and explain how the community helper serves the community. Continue in this same manner until several students have had a chance to give clues about different community helpers.

2. Give each student a copy of page 13. Read aloud the sentence starters and have each student complete the sentences for a different community helper. Then have each child draw a picture of himself dressed as this helper.

3. Compile the students' completed reproducibles between two construction-paper covers. Add a hand-shaped cut-out and the title "People Who Give A Helping Hand In The Community" to the front cover.

All About ______________________________

community helper

by ______________________________

student's name

1. This worker helps the community by ____________
____
____
____
______________________________.

2. This community helper works at ____________
______________________________.

3. While working this community helper uses
____
____
____
______________________________.

Here is a picture of myself dressed as this community helper.

How To Extend The Lesson:

- Have students make medallions for a variety of community helpers. On one side of a white construction-paper circle, have each student write the name of a desired community helper. Then have each student illustrate and personalize himself as this helper on the blank side of his circle. To complete his project, a student hole-punches the top of his cutout, threads a length of yarn through the hole, securely ties the yarn ends, and dangles the resulting medallion from his neck.

- Invite several community helpers—such as a firefighter, a police officer, and a veterinarian—to visit your classroom to speak to your students. Be sure to ask your students' parents and the school principal to share information about their jobs too!

- Pick and choose from the following three series of community helper books to share with your students.
  —In My Neighborhood Series (Kids Can Press)
  —If You Were A…Series (Benchmark Books)
  —Community Helpers Series (Bridgestone Books)

- Challenge students to write poems about their future career wishes. Post the poetry format shown and review it with your students. Next have each student refer to the format as he writes his poem on writing paper. Then set aside time for student volunteers to share their poems!

Line 1: "I wish I were"
Line 2: name of occupation
Line 3: where you would work
Line 4: description of your job
Line 5: "Happily"

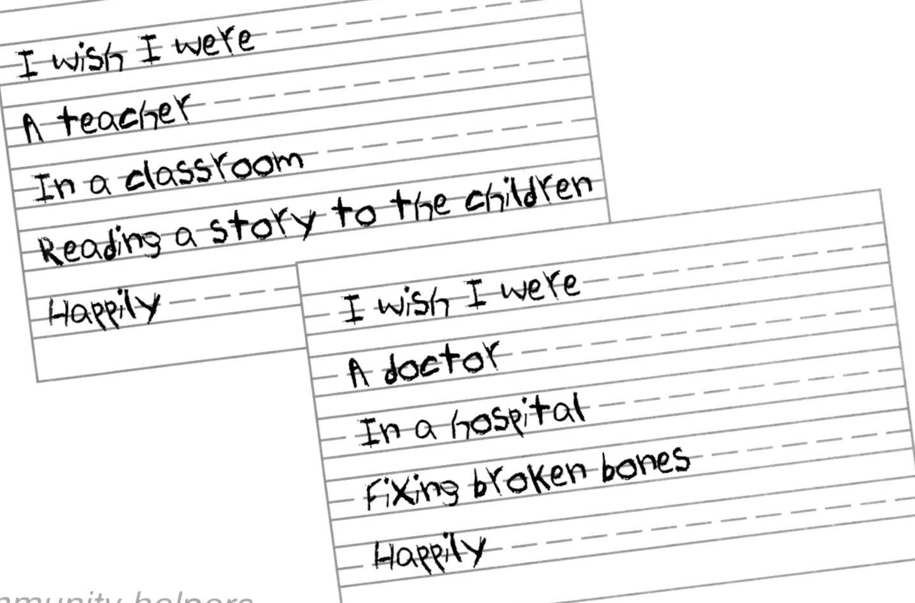

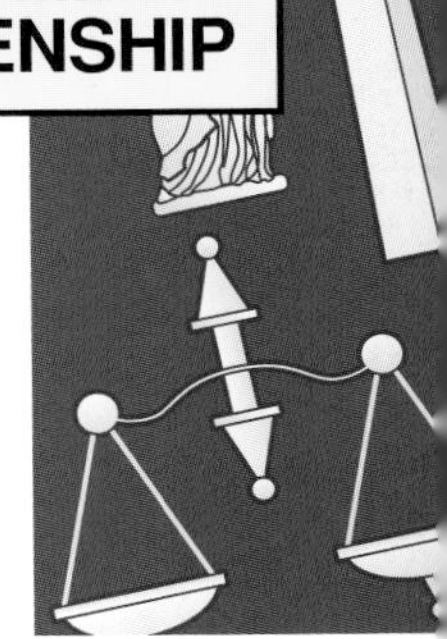

Know The Rules!

No doubt students will agree that following rules is cool—whether at home or at school!

Skill: Identifying the need for and use of rules at home and at school

Estimated Lesson Time: 35 minutes

Teacher Preparation:
Duplicate page 17 for each student.

Materials:
1 copy of page 17 per student
scissors
glue

Background Information:
Rules provide guidelines for behavior at places like home, school, and the playground. When individuals follow these rules, the groups to which they belong enjoy fair and safe environments for living, learning, and playing. By accepting the responsibility of following rules, children are rewarded with a happier and healthier community.

Introducing The Lesson:

Tell students that they are going to play the game Duck, Duck, Goose. In an open area of the classroom, gather students in a circle and have them sit on the floor. Then take the part of the Chooser and walk around the outside of the circle tapping students on their heads as you go. Purposely play the game a different way by naming items that belong to a category as you tap each child's head, rather than saying "duck." When you reach the child you want to choose, say a word that doesn't fit the category. Since the students won't know the rules to this game variation, this child won't know to jump up and chase you. At this point, appear baffled and ask students why they aren't playing the game. After hearing their responses, confirm that you changed the rules of the game.

Steps:

1. Lead students to realize that there are a set of rules that all players should follow to ensure that a game is played fairly. Explain to students the rules to your variation of Duck, Duck, Goose. If desired, play the variation again to show students how much smoother the game runs once all the players know the rules.

2. Explain to students that rules help people know what to do. Share the Background Information on page 15. Next ask students how rules maintain a peaceful classroom. Also ask students to describe how rules affect their home life.
3. Distribute a copy of page 17 to each student. Review the directions with students. Next have each child cut out the rules and set them aside. Then, in turn, read aloud each rule and have students glue it to the corresponding building (home or school).
4. Challenge students to complete the Bonus Box activity.
5. After students have completed the activity, read aloud each rule again and ask student volunteers to explain why the rule is needed.

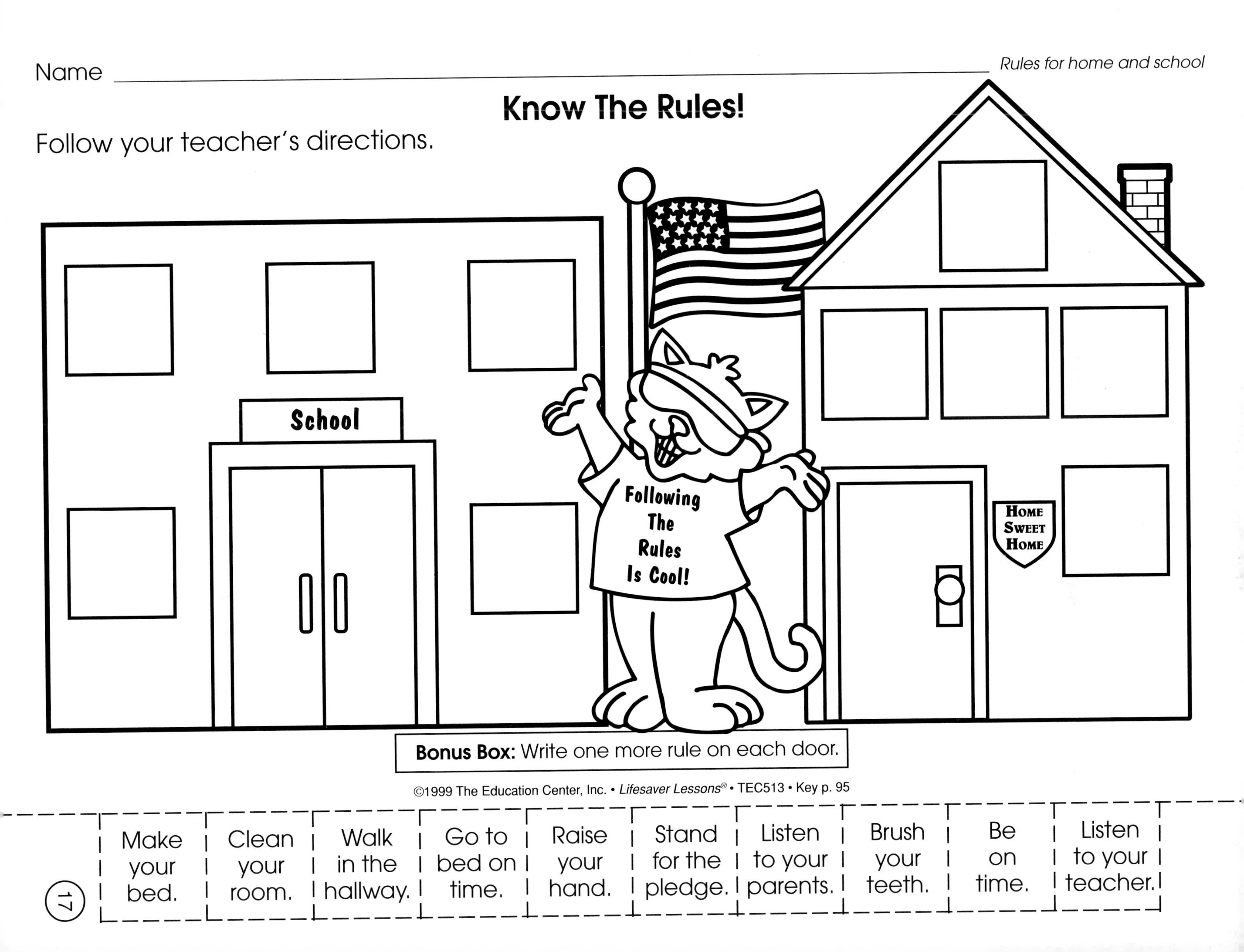
Name
Rules for home and school
Know The Rules!
Follow your teacher's directions.
School
Following The Rules Is Cool!
HOME SWEET HOME
Bonus Box: Write one more rule on each door.
©1999 The Education Center, Inc. • Lifesaver Lessons® • TEC513 • Key p. 95
Make your bed.
Clean your room.
Walk in the hallway.
Go to bed on time.
Raise your hand.
Stand for the pledge.
Listen to your parents.
Brush your teeth.
Be on time.
Listen to your teacher.
17

How To Extend The Lesson:

- Help students remember the rules for home and school with this little ditty.

Rules
(sung to the tune of "B-I-N-G-O")

Follow rules at home and school.
[Listen to your teacher.]
R-U-L-E-S
R-U-L-E-S
R-U-L-E-S
We follow all the rules.

Repeat the verse several times substituting other rules, such as *go to bed at bedtime, raise your hand to answer,* or *don't run in the hallway.*

- No doubt students will agree that all rules are important. But this critical-thinking activity gives students the chance to promote what they believe to be the most important rules at school. To begin, divide students into small groups. Ask each group to choose the school rule it believes is most important and discuss the reasons for the choice. After a predetermined amount of time, ask each group to share its choice and reasons.

- Review with students one of the most important rules of all with these good-as-gold badges. Discuss with students the Golden Rule: *Treat others the way you would like to be treated.* Then give each child a laminated, construction-paper copy of the badge shown below. Have each child use a permanent marker to write his name on the provided line. Then have him tape the badge to his desk or store it in his desk. Each time you see a child following the Golden Rule, attach a gold, self-adhesive star sticker to his badge. When a child has collected five stars, tape a large safety pin to the back of his badge and invite him to wear it with pride!

Follow The Rules Is Cool!

Official Member of the GOLDEN RULE CLUB

____
name

I treat others the way I'd like to be treated.

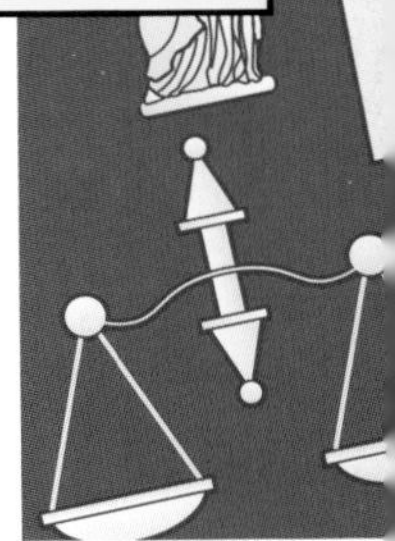

Boning Up On Good Citizenship

Dig into this character-building lesson that's sure to foster an understanding of citizenship and its importance in the classroom.

Skill: Identifying characteristics of a good classroom citizen

Estimated Lesson Time: 30 minutes

Teacher Preparation:
Duplicate page 21 for each student.

Materials:
1 copy of page 21 per student

Background Information:
- A *citizen* is a person who is a member of a special community or group of people.
- A person can be a citizen of a very large community like the United States, and a person can be a citizen of a smaller community like a classroom.
- To become a citizen, special requirements must be fulfilled. For example, a classroom citizen must be enrolled in a particular classroom, attend school regularly, and follow the established rules.

Introducing The Lesson:

Begin the lesson by congratulating your youngsters. Of course students will be curious as to why they are being congratulated. With grand fanfare, explain that each one of them has the honor of being a citizen of [room number]. Also explain that the honor comes with certain responsibilities, which they will discuss in the lesson.

Steps:

1. Use the Background Information on page 19 to provide students with information about citizenship.

2. Ask students to describe the characteristics of a good citizen. Write students' responses on the chalkboard. Explain to students that to be good citizens, they have the responsibility to carry out these favorable behaviors.

3. Next tell students that a new student named Dudley Doggie wants to join their class. Explain to students that Dudley wants to know what to do to be considered a good citizen in their classroom.

4. Give each student a copy of page 21. Read each phrase on the bottom half of the reproducible. Have each child mark a check in the box if the sentence describes a behavior of a good citizen. Next instruct students to cut out the sentences on the dotted lines and glue the sentences with checks in the provided area.

5. Challenge students to complete the Bonus Box activity.

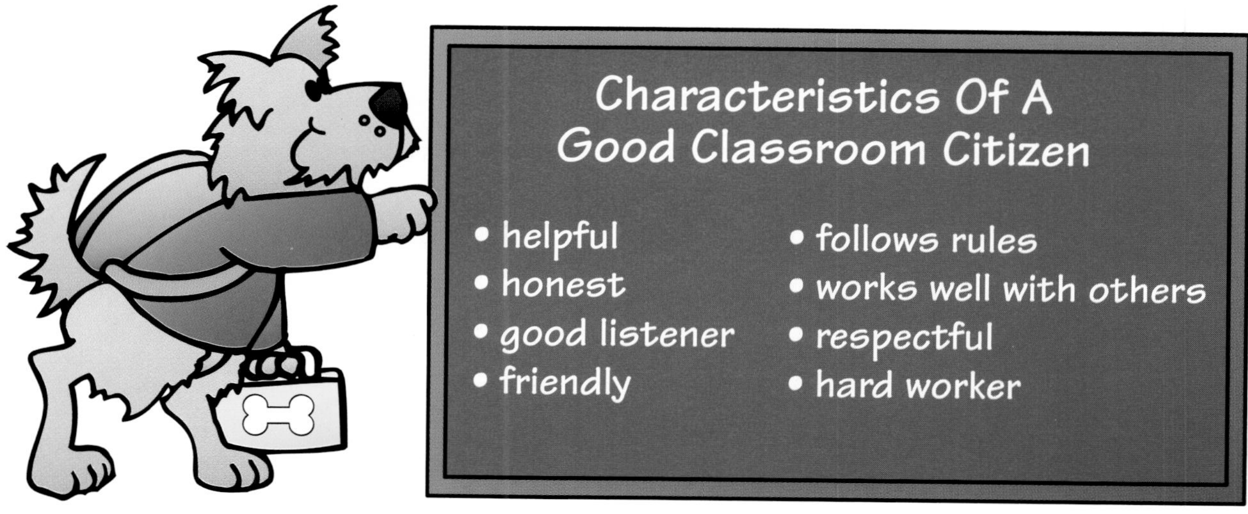

Name ____________________ *Identifying characteristics of a good classroom citizen*

Digging Into Good Citizenship

Teach Dudley Doggie about good citizenship in the classroom. Follow your teacher's directions.

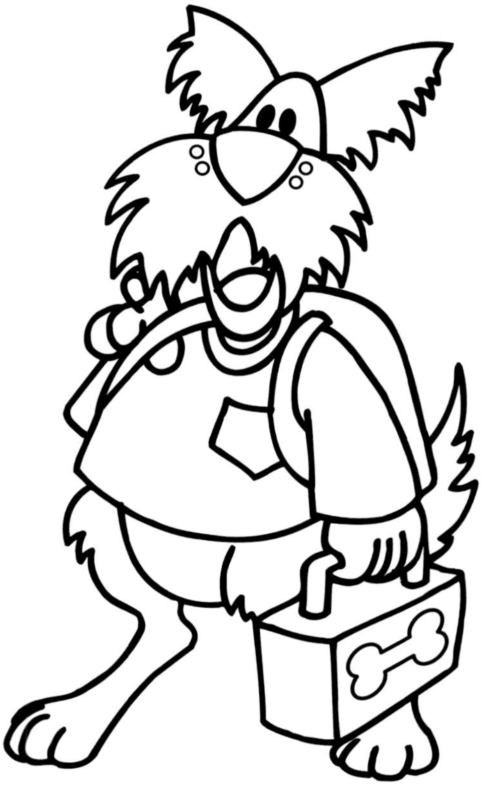

How To Be A Good Citizen:

Bonus Box: Think about a time when you helped a classmate. Draw a picture of this kind deed on the back of this paper.

☐ help others	☐ be a good listener
☐ keep your desk messy	☐ respect your teacher and classmates
☐ be a good sport	☐ never share
☐ be honest	☐ always try your best
☐ follow the rules	☐ be kind to your classmates

How To Extend The Lesson:

- Encourage good classroom citizens all year long with this class journal. Obtain a three-ring binder that has a clear pocket on the cover. Title an 8 1/2" x 11" sheet of paper “The Good Citizen Journal” and decorate it as desired. Slip the completed cover page inside the pocket. Also hole-punch several sheets of writing paper and store it in the binder; then place the binder in an easily accessible location. When a youngster sees a classmate exhibiting good citizenship, he goes to the journal, describes the incident on a sheet of provided paper, and signs his name and the date under the entry. At the end of each week, read aloud each new entry in the book.

- Promote good citizenship with these one-of-a-kind projects! Have each child draw a portrait of herself on a 7" x 10" sheet of white paper and glue it to a 9" x 12" sheet of colored construction paper. Next have her list words that describe a good citizen on a sheet of writing paper; then instruct her to attach this paper to the bottom of her portrait. Display the completed projects on a classroom wall titled “What Great Classroom Citizens!”

- Copy the Good Citizenship proclamation shown onto bulletin-board paper and post it on a classroom wall at a student’s level. Read the proclamation; then lead students in a review of good citizenship. Next ask each student to sign the proclamation. Then present each student with a personalized copy of the good citizenship badge below. No doubt students will be motivated to carry on good citizen habits!

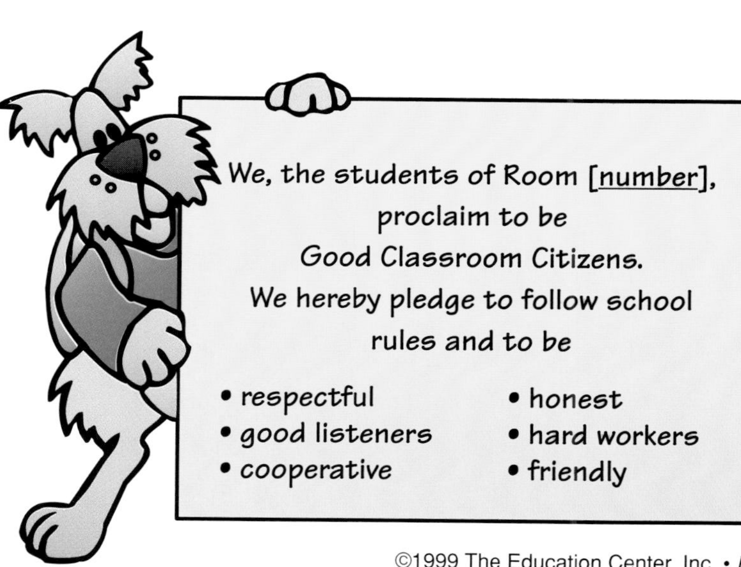

Badge

Hear Ye, Hear Ye!

Sign your youngsters up for a better understanding of their classroom rights and responsibilities with this lesson.

Skill: Understanding classroom rights and responsibilities

Estimated Lesson Time: 40 minutes

Teacher Preparation:
Duplicate page 25 for each student.

Materials:
1 copy of page 25 per student
2 sheets of chart paper
marker
scissors
glue

Background Information:

A *right* is a power or privilege that justly belongs to someone. Being a classroom citizen gives students certain rights. Some rights in the classroom include:

- the right to ask questions
- the right to be respected by classmates and teachers
- the right to have your own opinion
- the right to learn in a safe place
- the right to your own private space

A *responsibility* is something that a person has a duty to do. Students have many responsibilities in the classroom. Some responsibilities include:

- following rules
- listening to teachers and classmates
- respecting other people's privacy
- respecting other people's space
- keeping the classroom clean

Introducing The Lesson:

Stride to the front of the classroom and say, "Hear ye! Hear ye!" to get students' attention. Then ask your youngsters to imagine what school would be like if they didn't have the opportunity to ask questions, talk to their friends, or have their own private space. Invite student volunteers to share their thoughts. Next tell students that these are privileges, or *rights,* that they are allowed to have or do. Also explain that with these rights come responsibilities. Then tell students that they will be learning about their classroom rights and responsibilities today.

Classroom Rights

- to ask questions
- to learn
- to be heard
- to be safe
- to have private space

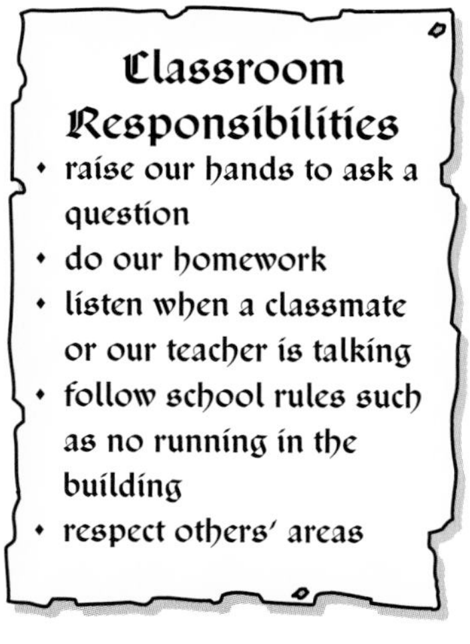

Classroom Responsibilities

- raise our hands to ask a question
- do our homework
- listen when a classmate or our teacher is talking
- follow school rules such as no running in the building
- respect others' areas

Steps:

1. Share with students the Background Information on page 23. Then provide students with some examples of rights and responsibilities. For example, students have the right to learn in a clean environment, so all students are responsible for cleaning up after themselves. Another example is that students have the right to be heard; therefore, students shouldn't talk when another classmate is talking to the class.

2. Ask students to brainstorm a list of classroom rights. Record their responses on a sheet of chart paper.

3. For each right on the chart, enlist students' help in identifying a responsibility. Write these responsibilities on a separate sheet of chart paper.

4. Ask students to sign both sheets of chart paper to acknowledge their rights and responsibilities. Post both sheets of chart paper in the classroom for students to refer to throughout the year.

5. Distribute a copy of page 25 to each student. Have each child write the class's room number on the provided line. Next read the directions aloud. Direct students to cut out the picture cards at the bottom of the page. Read aloud each right and have the student glue the corresponding responsibility in the provided box. Finally, have each child write an additional right on the lines.

Name ____________________

Hear Ye, Hear Ye!

Cut and glue to show how to use each right responsibly.

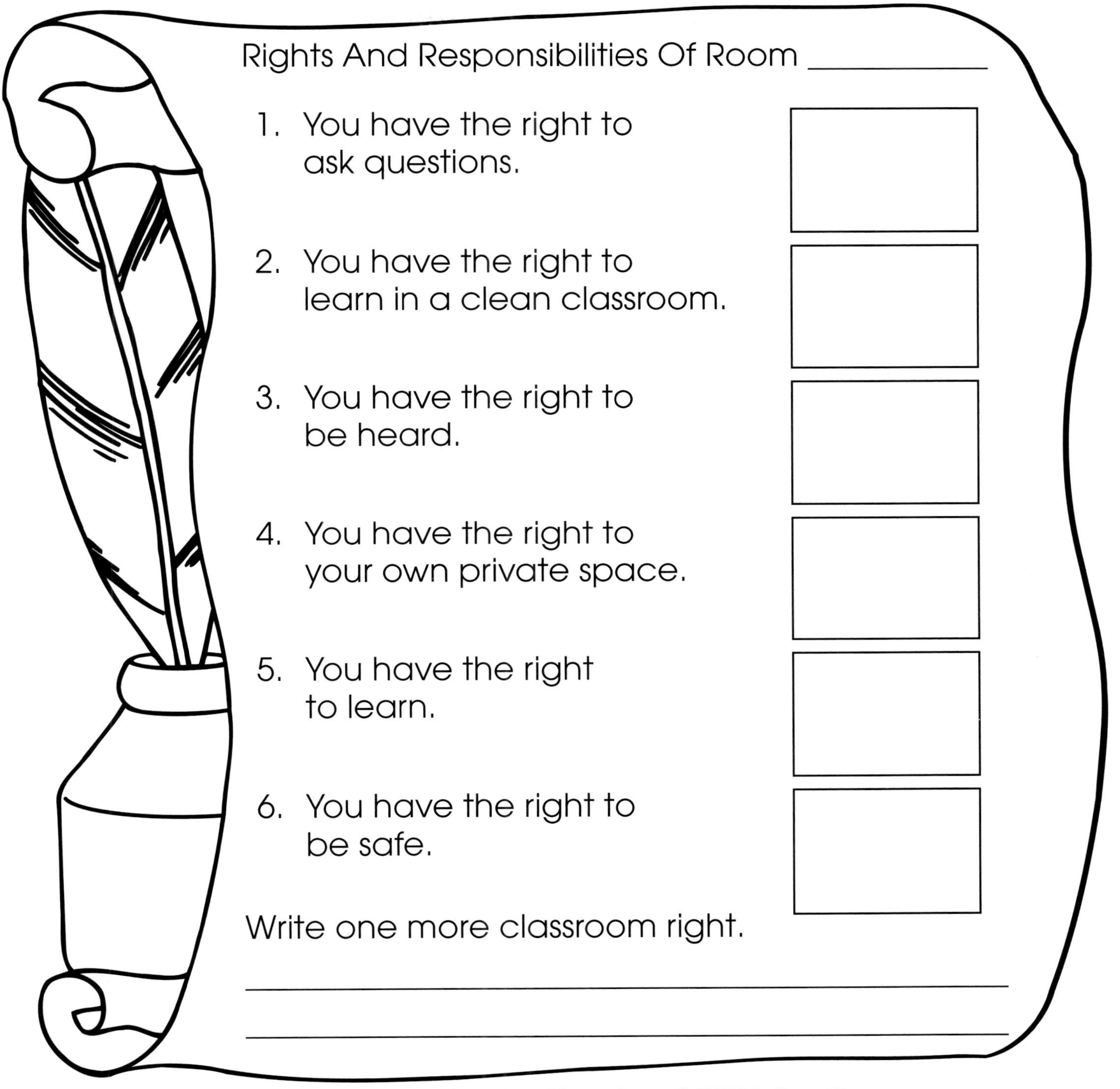

Rights And Responsibilities Of Room ________

1. You have the right to ask questions.
2. You have the right to learn in a clean classroom.
3. You have the right to be heard.
4. You have the right to your own private space.
5. You have the right to learn.
6. You have the right to be safe.

Write one more classroom right.

____

____

How To Extend The Lesson:

- Have students make bookmarks to help them remember their classroom rights and responsibilities. Give each child a 3" x 7" piece of light-colored construction paper. Have each child title one side of the paper "Classroom Rights." Then direct her to list at least five of her classroom rights under the title. Next have her flip her bookmark and title this side "Classroom Responsibilities." Ask her to write at least five responsibilities under this title. Finally have her add an eye-catching border to each side of the resulting bookmark. As students use their bookmarks throughout the school year, classroom rights and responsibilities are sure to reviewed.

- Once your youngsters have an understanding of rights, an activity on limits is surely in order! Explain to students that although some actions may seem fun to the person who does them, these actions may not be okay with the people around him. Tell students that rights have *limits,* or boundaries, that you do not go beyond. For example, you might have the right to color a picture at school, but only when the teacher says that it is free time or art time. If you are coloring a picture when you are supposed to be doing a math assignment, then you have gone beyond your limits. Encourage students to share additional examples of limits. If desired, write their responses on a stop sign–shaped cutout titled "Know Your Limits!"

- Duplicate several copies of the award pattern shown below. Place the patterns in a container along with scissors, tape, and crayons. When a student spots another student using a classroom right in a responsible manner, he decorates the award, cuts it out, and then tapes it to the shirt of the deserving student.

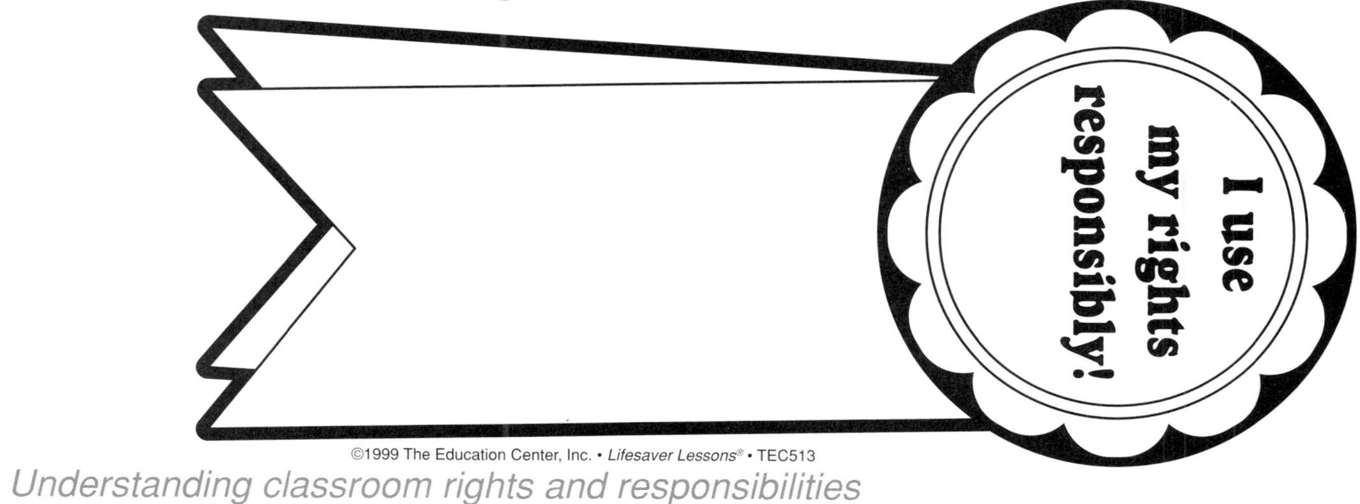

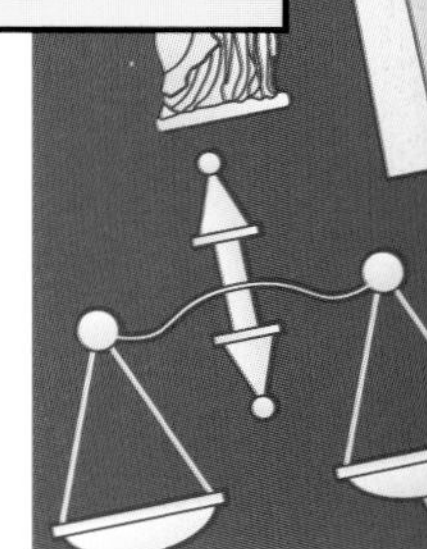

Take A Vote!

Gain your youngsters' vote of approval with this winning lesson!

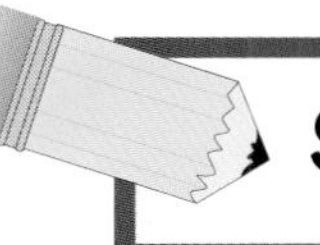

Skill: Participating in democratic decision making

Estimated Lesson Time: 45 minutes

Teacher Preparation:

1. Duplicate page 29 for each student.
2. Gather two books appropriate for storytime.

Materials:

1 copy of page 29 per student
two children's books

Background Information:

With democratic decision making, any person who meets voter requirements may *vote,* or make choices, not just a select few or a single person.

Introducing The Lesson:

Tell students that you would like their help in deciding which book to read at storytime. Name the two choices and show students the covers of the books. Next ask students to think about the best way to decide which book to read. Ask questions such as "Would it be fair if just one student decided?", "Would it be fair if just the girls made the decision?", and "Would it be fair if only students with brown hair decided?" Lead students to realize that the only fair way to decide which book to read is to take a vote.

Steps:

1. Share with students the Background Information on page 27. Explain to students that with democratic decision making each person has a chance to make her opinion known. The issue is usually put to a vote. The choice with the most votes wins.

2. Announce each book title and ask each student to raise her hand to vote for the book of her choice. Tally students' votes on the chalkboard. Enlist students' help in counting the tally marks to determine which book wins. Discuss whether or not this process was a fair way to make a decision. Then set aside the winning book to read at storytime.

3. Distribute a copy of page 29 to each student. On the chalkboard, write the topic of the next election (see the list to the left for suggestions). Also write up to three choices for the topic. Have each student copy the topic and choices on the provided lines. In turn, ask each child to announce her vote. Have each child tally the results on her sheet while you do the same on the chalkboard. After students have voted, have them count the tally marks and record the number of votes for each choice. Then have students complete the remainder of the reproducible.

Name ______________________________ *Participating in democratic decision making*

Let's Vote!

Follow your teacher's directions.

Tally Sheet Topic ______________________________	
Choices:	Tally:
1.	
2.	
3.	

Count the tallies. Complete.

________ students voted for Choice #1.

________ students voted for Choice #2.

________ students voted for Choice #3.

The majority of students voted for Choice #________ .

Do you think this voting process was a fair way to make a decision?
Why or why not? ______________________________

____

____

____

How To Extend The Lesson:

- Explain to students that although voting for elected officials is a right in the United States, voters must meet certain requirements to vote in an election. A voter must be 18 years of age or older, a citizen of the United States, and registered. Although your youngsters are not of age to vote in an actual election, they'll enjoy registering to vote in a mock election. Explain that people register to vote and their names are added to a list of eligible voters. Give each child a copy of the registration form shown below and help him complete it as needed. Then collect the forms and keep them on file. Next time your class votes on an issue, have students present their voter registration cards prior to voting.

- Explain to students that many years ago only wealthy white men were allowed to vote. In time, though, each group won its right to participate in the democracy. However, some people choose not to voice their opinions even though they have the right to vote. Discuss with students the importance of voting, rather than letting others make these decisions for them. Then, on story paper, have each child write about the importance of voting. Ask that she include a pledge to vote once she turns 18. Finally direct her to illustrate herself (at the age of 18) voting.

Name ____________________

Date Of Birth ____________________ Age __________

Address ____________________

____

Signature ____________________

A Salute To United States Symbols

Turn your young patriots into real Yankee Doodle dandies with this star-spangled salute to important symbols of our country.

Skill: Identifying United States symbols

Estimated Lesson Time: 45 minutes

Teacher Preparation:

1. Duplicate page 33 for each student plus one extra.
2. Cut out the symbols on the bottom of the extra reproducible.

Materials:

1 copy of page 33 per student plus one extra
scissors
glue

Background Information:

- **The U.S. flag** has 13 stripes to represent the original 13 colonies and 50 stars to represent the current 50 states. The flag is a symbol of the people, government, and ideas of our country. It has been given many different names, such as the *Stars and Stripes,* the *Star-Spangled Banner,* and *Old Glory.*
- **The Statue of Liberty** was given to the United States from the people of France to honor 100 years of independence. It is a symbol of freedom to the millions of immigrants entering America.
- **The Liberty Bell,** a symbol of American independence, was rung on July 8, 1776, to announce the adoption of the Declaration of Independence.
- **The bald eagle,** found only in North America, is the national bird of the United States. This bird is known for its strength, and it represents the power of our country.
- **The White House** is the official residence and workplace of our country's president.
- **Uncle Sam** is a fictitious character who symbolizes the United States. The costume of Uncle Sam, decorated with stars and stripes, was created in the 1830s and 1840s.
- **The Pledge of Allegiance** is a solemn promise of loyalty to the United States. It is often recited while saluting the flag.
- **The Great Seal of the United States** is a symbol of the United States that is used on official documents.

Introducing The Lesson:

Review with your students that symbols can be used to show pride. Use your school mascot (or logo) as an example. Discuss with students why they think people at their school might have clothing, pencils, or bumper stickers featuring the school mascot. Lead students to understand that when people show these symbols at school events it expresses that they are proud to be part of that school. Then tell students that people also use symbols to show that they are proud to be citizens of the United States.

Steps:

1. Explain to students that all countries have symbols that are meaningful to them. The United States has several symbols that represent our country. These symbols make us feel proud to be Americans.

2. Distribute a copy of page 33 to each student. Have students refer to the pictures cards at the bottom of the page as you share the Background Information (page 31) about each symbol.

3. Explain the directions (shown to the left) for the activity. Then pair students and have them follow the rules to complete the activity. If desired, have student pairs repeat the activity for extra practice.

4. When game time is over, have each student glue the United States symbols to the boxes on the gameboard.

5. Challenge students to complete the Bonus Box activity.

Directions:

- Give each player a copy of page 33, scissors, a pencil, and glue.
- Each player cuts out the symbol cards at the bottom of the page. He then shuffles his cards and places them facedown in front of him.
- Player 1 turns over his top card. If the card shows a symbol of the United States, he places it on the flag. If the card does not show a U.S. symbol, the player places the card in his discard pile, and it is Player 2's turn.
- Player 2 turns over his top card and takes his turn as did Player 1.
- Play continues until one player has placed a U.S. symbol on each box on the flag.

Name ________________________________

A Salute To United States Symbols

Follow your teacher's directions.

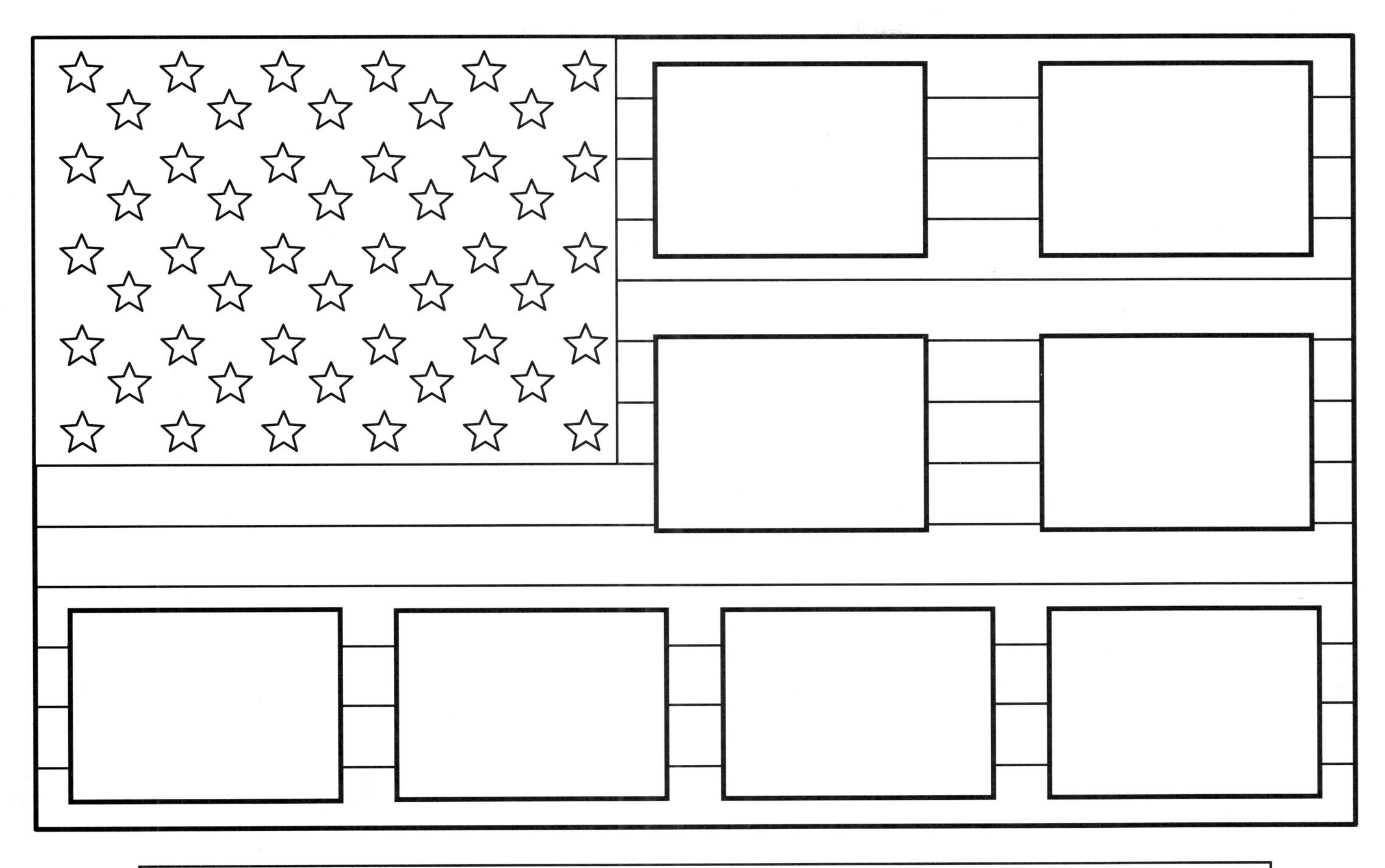

Bonus Box: On the back of this paper, write about your favorite U.S. symbol.

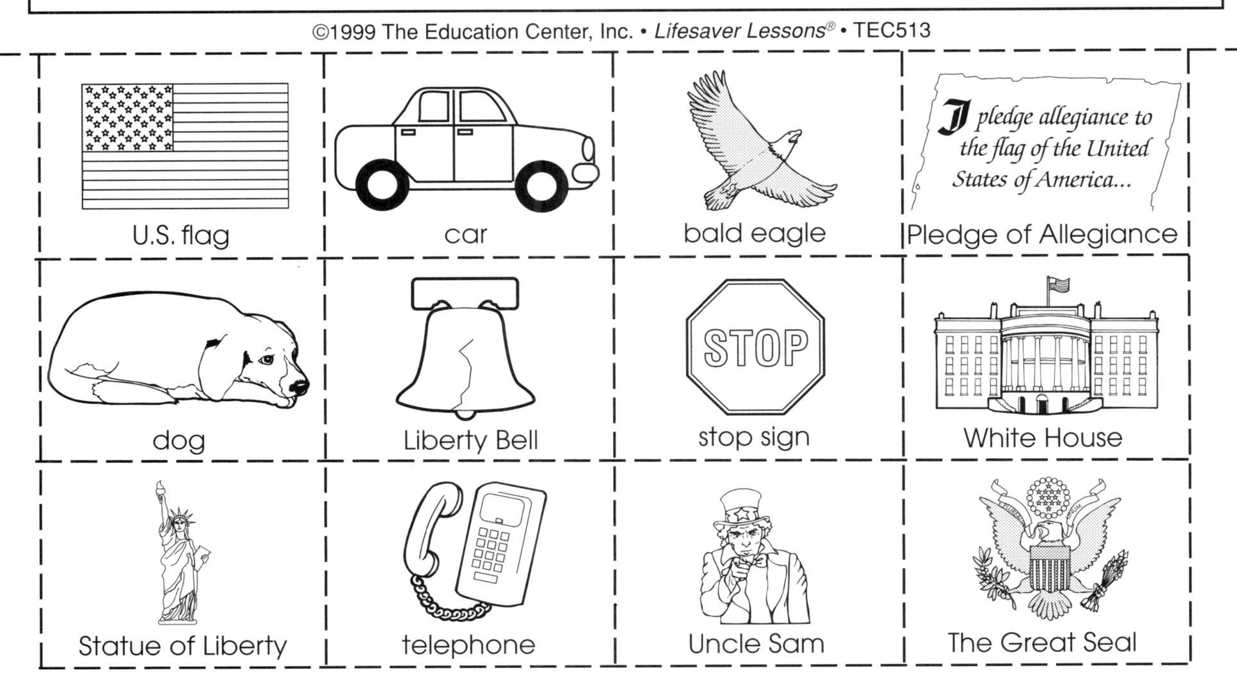

How To Extend The Lesson

- Take time to share some of these patriotic books with your youngsters.
  — *The Statue Of Liberty* by Lucille Recht Penner (Random House, Inc.; 1995)
  — *The Flag We Love* by Pam Muñoz Ryan (Charlesbridge Publishing, Inc.; 1996)
  — *Red, White, And Blue: The Story Of The American Flag* by John Herman (Grosset & Dunlap, 1998)
  — *American Too* by Elisa Bartone (Lothrop, Lee & Shepard Books; 1996)
  — *America The Beautiful* by Katharine Lee Bates (Atheneum, 1993)

- Promote American pride with a top ten list. As a class, brainstorm the best things about the United States. Write students' ideas on the chalkboard. Then, by student vote, determine the students' top ten ideas. Copy the resulting list onto a length of white bulletin-board paper labeled "Ten Best Things About Living In The United States." Have students use red or blue markers to autograph the outer edges of the resulting poster; then display it in the hallway for everyone to see!

- Hold a special "Celebrate America" day that your students plan themselves! Several days prior to the event, invite each student to submit ideas for the celebration. Ideas might include dressing in red, white, and blue; writing with only red or blue colored pencils and chalk; drawing pictures of what American pride means; and singing songs such as "Yankee Doodle" and "This Land Is Your Land." Once all the ideas have been submitted, share them with students and enlist their help in determining the order of the day's events. Then, on the special day, just follow the predetermined plan. For added fun, salute your little patriots for a job well done with a serving of patriotic punch. (See the recipe to the left.)

Patriotic Punch

Ingredients and supplies needed for each student:

3/4 cup red punch
1 scoop vanilla frozen yogurt
4 blueberries, rinsed

one 9-oz. plastic cup
1 straw
ice-cream scoop

Place a scoop of yogurt in the cup. Pour the punch over the yogurt. Add the blueberries. Place the straw in the cup and enjoy!

A Trip To The Zoo

An imaginary trip to the zoo is the perfect place for students to go wild over map symbols!

Skill: Using map symbols

Estimated Lesson Time: 30 minutes

Teacher Preparation:
Duplicate page 37 for each student.

Materials:
1 copy of page 37 per student
scissors
glue
crayons

Background Information:
Map symbols are pictures that stand for places that are too big to be drawn on a map. Since map symbols are not the same on every map, most maps have a list called a *key* or *legend* to show what each symbol on the map means. Mapmakers usually use the same colors to represent the same things. For example, water is usually blue and forests are usually green.

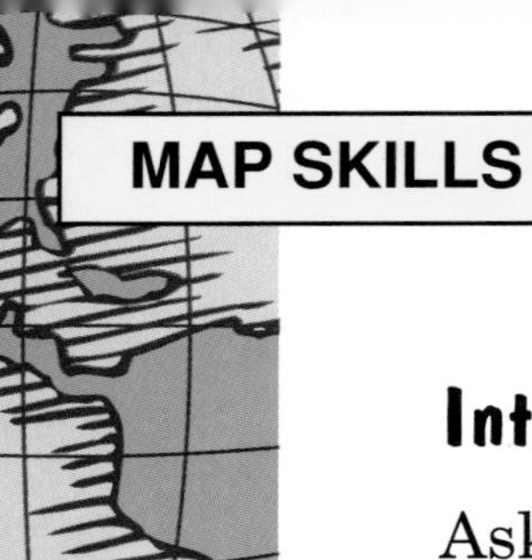

Introducing The Lesson:

Ask students who have been to the zoo to share their favorite exhibits. Then ask students who have never been to the zoo which exhibit they think they would visit first if they were at the zoo. Next tell students that some zoos are really large. Ask students how they might find the exhibit they want to visit first. Guide students to realize that a map of the zoo would be very helpful. Then tell students that they will be working with a zoo map today.

Steps:

1. Draw a simple tree and a lake on the chalkboard and ask students to tell what each represents. Label each picture. Then explain that simple drawings, or *symbols,* are used to represent actual objects on a map.

2. Draw a box around the two symbols and label the box "Map Key." Share the Background Information about map keys on page 35.

3. Distribute a copy of page 37 to each student. Review with students the map key on the page. Then have each child color and cut out the symbols at the bottom of the page. Next read aloud each word clue on the map. Instruct each child to put a drop of glue on each dot. Then have her refer to the map key as she glues each symbol in place.

4. Challenge students to complete the Bonus Box activity.

5. After students complete their maps, announce each object on the map key and have students find the location on their maps.

Name ______________________ *Using map symbols*

A Trip To The Zoo

Follow your teacher's directions.

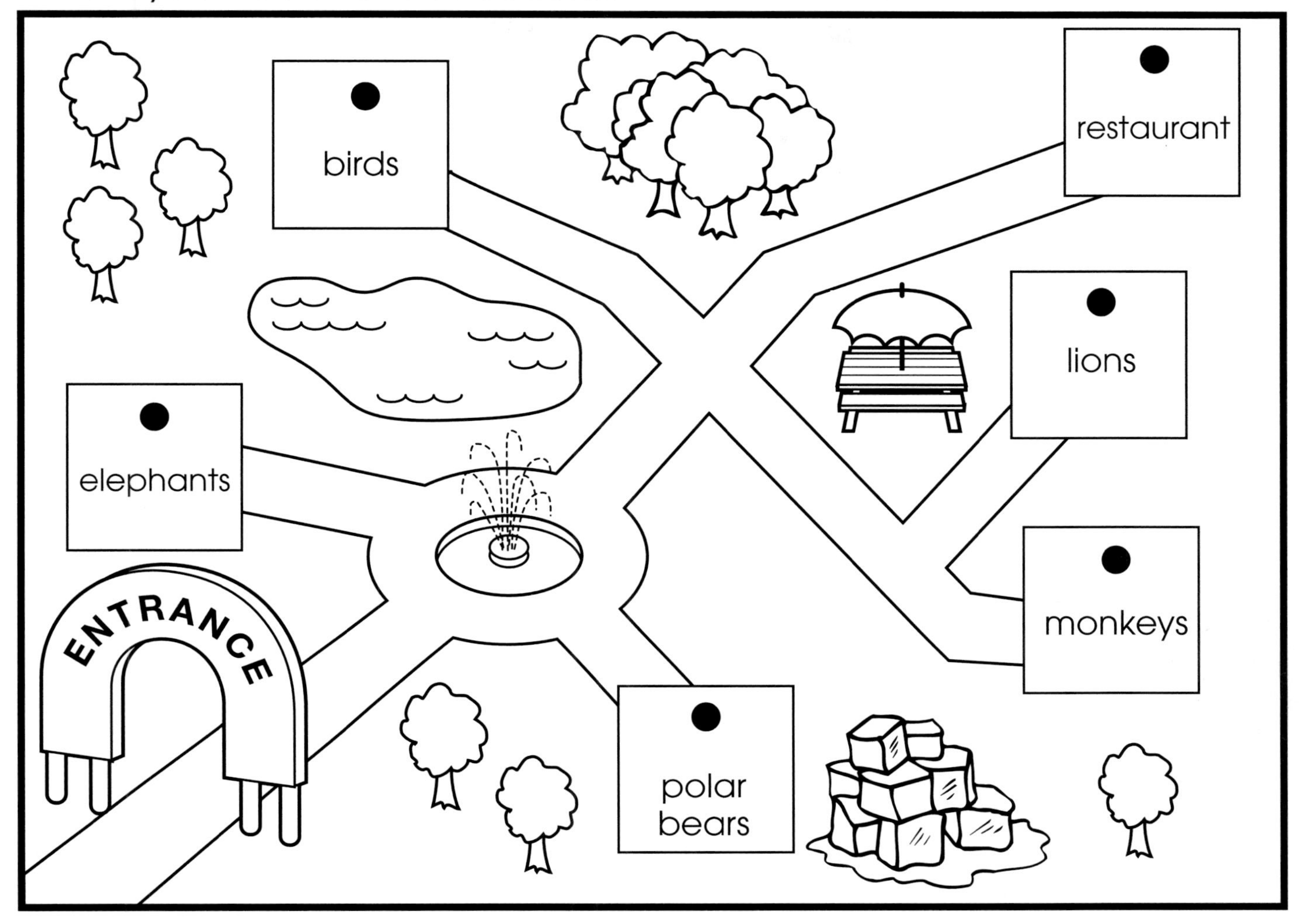

Bonus Box: Color each symbol on the map key to match the symbols on the map.

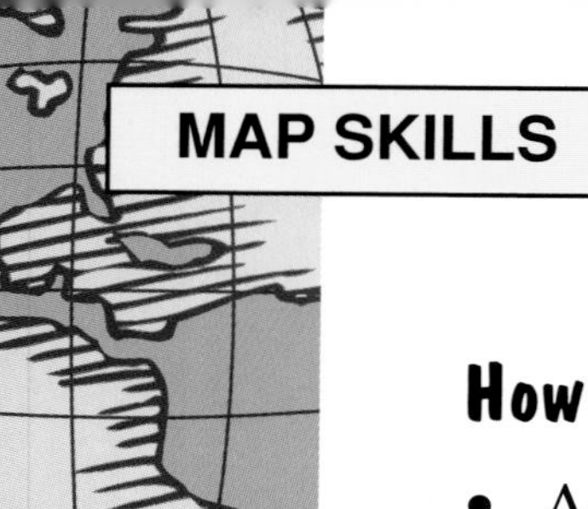

How To Extend The Lesson:

- Ask each child to create her own symbols for other places at a zoo, such as the ticket office; the bathroom; the gift store; and the giraffe, fish, bear, and reptile exhibits. Then, as students share their work, encourage them to notice the similarities and differences in their symbols.

- This two-person memory game is sure to be a good match for your youngsters. To prepare, use discarded magazines to cut out pictures of objects such as stores, churches, restaurants, bodies of water, parks, and hospitals. Glue each picture to an index card. Then, for each picture, draw a simple symbol on a different index card that corresponds to the picture. To play, a child shuffles the cards and places them facedown on the playing surface. Player One turns over two cards. If the two cards match (a symbol and a matching picture), she keeps both cards and takes another turn. If the cards do not match, she returns them to their facedown position and Player Two takes his turn. Play continues in this manner until all the cards have been matched. The player with the most cards wins!

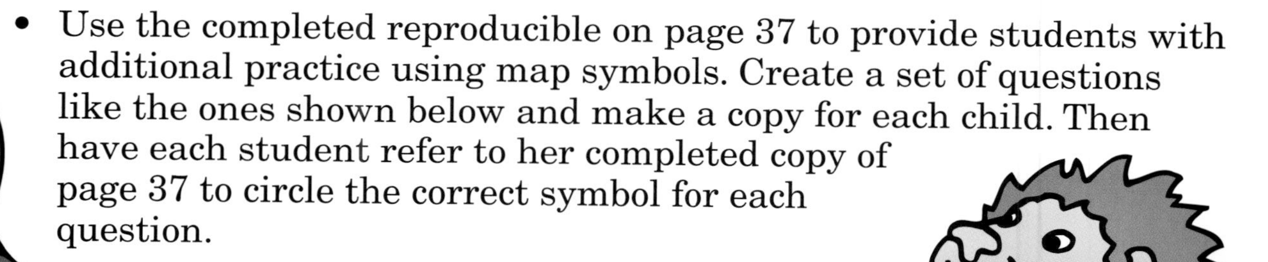

- Use the completed reproducible on page 37 to provide students with additional practice using map symbols. Create a set of questions like the ones shown below and make a copy for each child. Then have each student refer to her completed copy of page 37 to circle the correct symbol for each question.

Classroom Construction

Roll up your sleeves and begin building map skills with this lesson that gives youngsters a bird's-eye view of their classroom!

Skill: Creating a classroom map

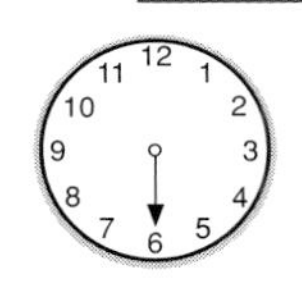

Estimated Lesson Time: 30 minutes

Teacher Preparation:

1. Duplicate page 41 for each student. Extra copies may be needed if there are more items in your classroom than the number provided on the reproducible.
2. On the chalkboard draw a quick sketch (like the one shown) of Buddy the Bird.

Materials:

1 copy of page 41 per student
(extras may be needed)
1 sheet of drawing paper per student
crayons
scissors
glue
stapler

Background Information:

Most maps are flat drawings of places as seen from above. A map drawing provides a view of a particular place as if you were looking down on it from high above. Although you can see more the higher you go, everything looks smaller. When mapmakers draw maps, they decide what to include based on who will use them and why they need them. Maps only show things that are always there. For example, maps do not show people or objects that might move frequently, such as bicycles.

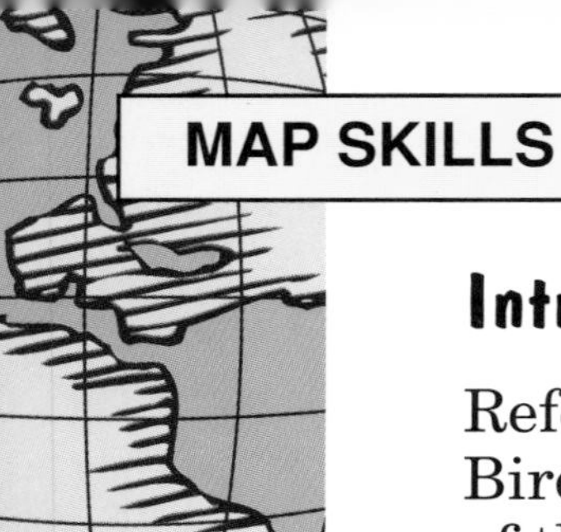

Introducing The Lesson:

Refer students to the chalkboard as you introduce them to Buddy the Bird. Ask each child to imagine that Buddy is flying around the ceiling of the classroom. Ask students to name some things Buddy might see from his overhead view. Then tell students that although Buddy can see the same objects they see, he sees them from a different view—a bird's-eye view. Explain that this view is the same view used when observing or making maps.

Steps:

1. Share the Background Information on page 39 with students. Next, place a stapler on a table. Have small groups of students view the stapler at the level of the table. Then place the stapler on the floor and have students look down at it. After each group has looked at the stapler from both views, discuss how the stapler looks different from each perspective.

2. Have students make maps of the classroom from Buddy's view. Distribute a copy of page 41, a sheet of drawing paper, scissors, crayons, and glue to each child. Explain to students that some of the items on the reproducible might not be needed on their classroom maps. (It depends on what is in their classroom.)

3. Share the directions below for creating a classroom map.
   - Color the symbols in the map key.
   - Color the larger symbols on the page to match the symbols in the map key.
   - Cut out the map key and the large symbols.
   - Glue the map key to the top right-hand corner of the drawing paper and write the room number beside the key.
   - Arrange the symbol cutouts to indicate where the items are located in the classroom; then glue them in place.

4. After students have completed their maps, ask each child to draw a star on her desk.

Patterns

Use with Steps 2, 3, and 4 on page 40.

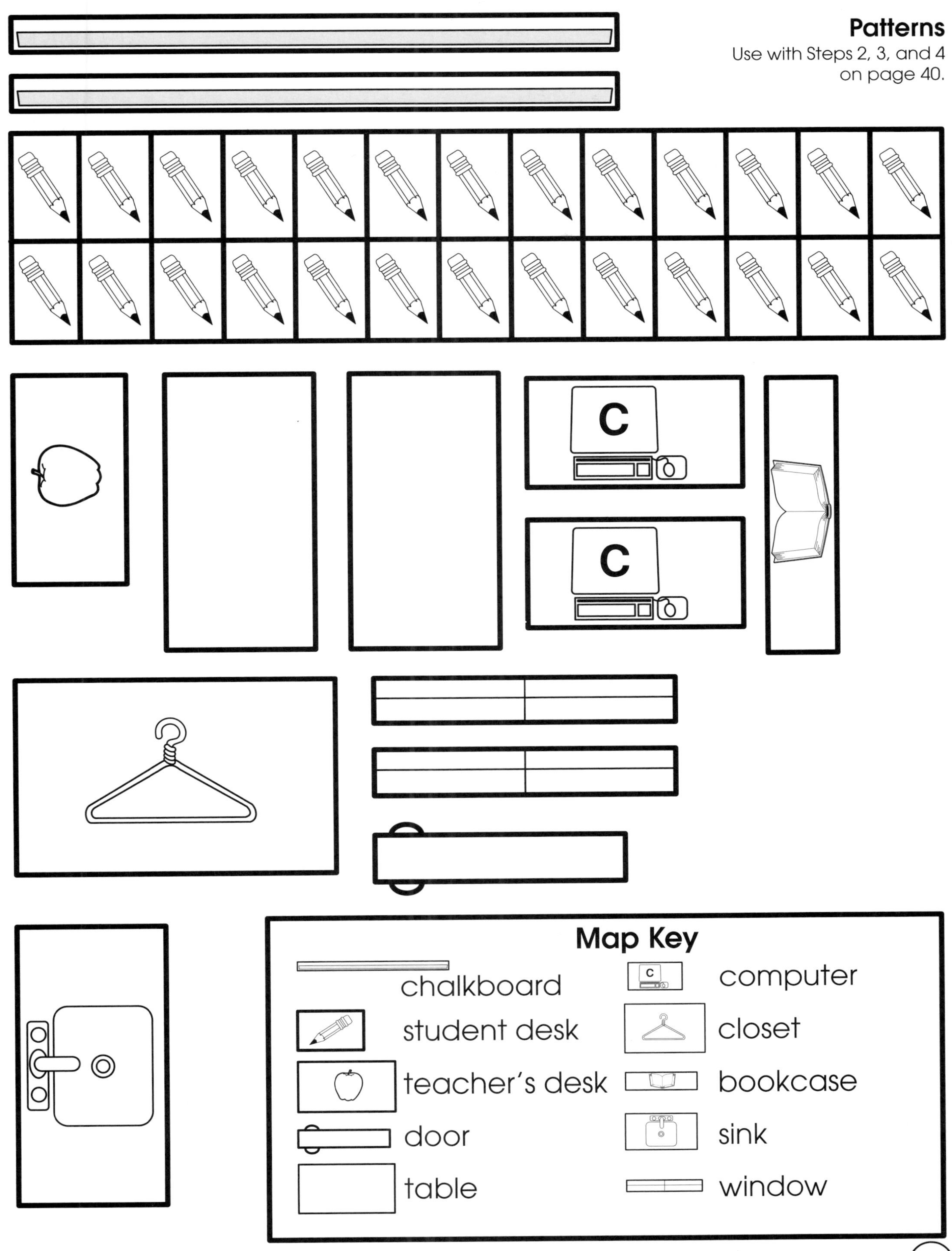

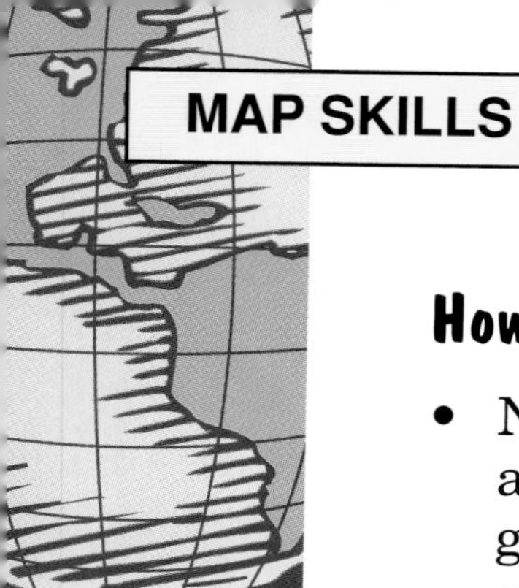

How To Extend The Lesson:

- Now that students have mapped their classroom, invite them to create maps showing new classroom arrangements. Give each small group of students a copy of page 41 and have them work together to glue the items on a sheet of blank paper to indicate how they would like the classroom set up. Then, throughout the remainder of the school year, pick a different map each month and enlist students' help in rearranging the room to match it. Post the map in a prominent classroom location along with a picture of the young mapmakers.
- Challenge students to create maps of their bedrooms. To do this, each child draws a map of his room on drawing paper. Ask that students use map symbols to show a variety of items in the room and design a matching map key. When the projects are complete, pair students and have each student take his partner on a guided tour of his room!
- Share the following literature with your youngsters. You'll find that these books are just the foundation you need to build better mapping skills.
  — *As The Crow Flies: A First Book Of Maps* by Gail Hartman (Aladdin Paperbacks, 1993)
  — *Me On The Map* by Joan Sweeney (Crown Publishers, Inc.; 1996)
- Present students with personalized construction-paper copies of the award shown below.

Shiver Me Maps!

Yo-ho-ho, mateys! Your adventure-seeking buccaneers will find this mapping lesson irresistible!

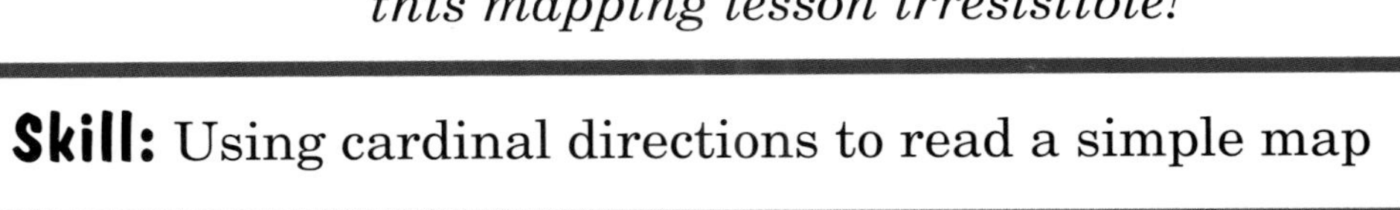

Skill: Using cardinal directions to read a simple map

Estimated Lesson Time: 45 minutes

Teacher Preparation:

1. Duplicate a copy of page 45 for each student.
2. Copy the map shown on page 44 onto your chalkboard.
3. Label each wall in your classroom with the corresponding cardinal direction.

Materials:

1 copy of page 45 per student
crayons
globe

Background Information:

Most maps have a direction finder, or a *compass rose,* to show the four main directions: north, south, east, and west. On a compass rose, *N* means north, *S* means south, *E* means east, and *W* means west. While all compass roses are not alike (some are labeled with words, some letters, and some only with the letter *N*), they all provide the same valuable information. On most maps, north is at the top of the page, as if the person reading the map is facing north. If a map does not have a compass rose, you usually can assume that north is at the top of the page.

A compass needle is a tiny magnet that always points north. The needle is pulled in this direction by the earth's magnetic forces. With a compass and a map, you can easily determine the direction you need to take to reach your destination. To do this, place a compass on a map and turn the map around until the north arrow on the map points in the same direction as the compass needle.

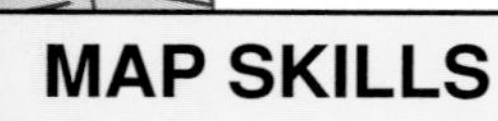

Introducing The Lesson:

Ask students to stand and face different directions. Then announce a command such as "Everyone face the teacher's desk." Next ask students whether the class across the hall would be facing in the same direction if they faced their teacher's desk. Tell students that perhaps they would but not necessarily. The teacher's desk may be in a different location from your desk. Then explain to students that there is a way that everyone in the school, as well as all over the earth, could face the same direction. Then, as you draw a compass rose on the chalkboard, tell students that the cardinal directions *(north, south, east,* and *west)* are standard direction words used around the world.

Steps:

1. Explain that north is always in the same direction, no matter where you are. Show students a globe and point out that north is the direction going toward the top of the globe. Then show students the directions of south, east, and west on the globe. Lead students to realize that north and south are opposite directions, and that east and west are opposite directions.

2. Tell students that cardinal directions make maps usable. Share with students the Background Information on page 43. Then point out the cardinal directions labeled on the classroom walls. Ask students to face north. Explain that when facing north, east is to the right and west is to the left. Then announce the other three directions and ask students to face each direction in turn.

3. Refer students to the compass rose and the map on the chalkboard. Ask students several map-related questions that involve cardinal directions. Questions might include "What direction must you go to get from the treasure chest to the palm tree?" or "What direction must you go to get from the shark to the cave?"

4. Distribute a copy of page 45 to each student. Review with students how to complete the reproducible.

5. Challenge students to complete the Bonus Box activity.

Name ____________________ *Using cardinal directions*

Treasure Island

Look at the map.
Color each item.

1. What is west of the ? green
2. What is east of the ? red
3. What is south of the ? brown
4. What is north of the ? yellow
5. Draw yourself east of the .

Write the direction word that tells which way to go to get from one place to the other.

6. from the to the ____________________
7. from the to the ____________________
8. from the to the ____________________

Bonus Box: On the back of this sheet, draw your own treasure island. Write three sentences telling how to get to different places on the island. Use direction words.

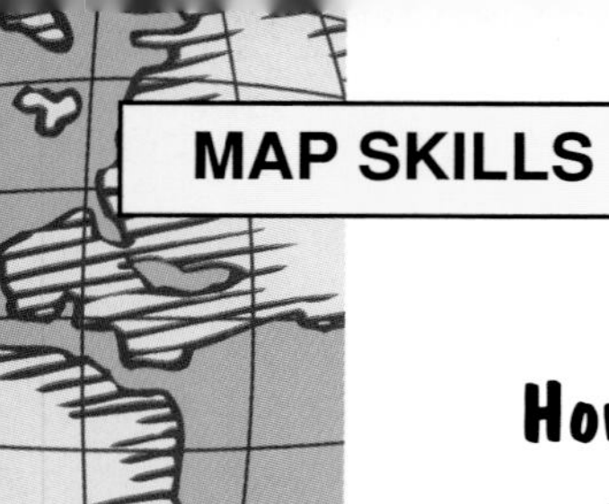

How To Extend The Lesson:

- Reinforce direction skills with this game! Ask a student volunteer to stand beside her desk. Secretly determine a mystery object in the classroom; then guide the student to the mystery object by giving her a series of clues. For example, you might announce clues such as "Take four giant steps north. Now take two tiny steps east." Continue giving clues until the student arrives at and identifies the object. Then invite another student to take a turn.

- Add excitement to map skills with a treasure hunt! For each of several small groups, hide a treasure (such as pencils, stickers, or sugarless gum) within the classroom. On a sheet of paper, write clues that include cardinal directions for how to find the treasure. Then divide students into groups and give each group a set of clues. Have students follow their clues to find their treasures.

- This whole-group activity is perfect for reviewing cardinal directions! Duplicate a one-inch grid, with approximately 25 squares, for each student. Have each child label the cardinal directions on his grid paper, then randomly mark an X on any square. Next have each child place a game marker on any square except for where the X is located. Randomly announce directions, such as "Move two spaces west," or "Move one space north." Each student moves his marker as directed. The first student to reach his X wins!

- Present each student with a personalized copy of the badge shown below.

Hooray For Holidays!

Students identify holiday symbols from various cultures in a lesson that's just right for any season!

Skill: Identifying holiday symbols

Estimated Lesson Time: 30 minutes

Teacher Preparation:

1. Duplicate page 49 for each student plus one extra.
2. Cut out the symbol cards on the extra copy of the reproducible and place them in a container.

Materials:

1 copy of page 49 per student plus one extra copy
15 game markers per student
container (for the symbol cards)
glue
scissors

Background Information:

The following list includes just a sampling of the many holidays celebrated throughout the world. It also includes one symbol associated with each holiday.

- **Mardi Gras:** a two-week celebration that ends the day before Ash Wednesday. A *king cake* is an oval ring of baked dough that has a small plastic doll hidden inside. The person who finds the doll in his piece of cake is king for the day.
- **Chinese New Year:** the most important holiday of the year for the Chinese. *Firecrackers* are set off because loud noises are thought to scare off evil spirits.
- **Hanukkah:** an eight-day Jewish celebration recalling the miracle of the oil and the victory for religious freedom. *A menorah* is a special candleholder that has eight candles (one for each night of Hanukkah) plus a helper candle.
- **Kwanzaa:** a weeklong celebration of the values and traditions of the Black American culture. The *mazao* is a bowl of fruits and vegetables that represents the harvest and the rewards of collective labor.
- **Passover:** an eight-day celebration of the Jews' rescue from slavery in Egypt. *Matzoh* is unleavened bread. It is the only bread that can be eaten during this holiday.
- **May Day:** a celebration of the arrival of spring that takes place on May 1. A *maypole* is a pole with colorful ribbons hung from its top. People hold the ends of the ribbons and dance around the maypole in such a way that the ribbons are woven into a pattern as the dance progresses.
- **Los Posadas:** a Mexican tradition beginning on December 16 in which groups of friends visit each other's houses and reenact Mary and Joseph's search for shelter preceding the birth of Jesus. A *piñata* is a party game for children that is held throughout the holiday.
- **Mother's Day:** a day to honor mothers. On the first national observance of this holiday, *carnations* were worn to honor mothers at the urging of Anna Jarvis, who started the campaign for Mother's Day.

Introducing The Lesson:

Draw a picture of a candy cane on the chalkboard. Ask students to identify the picture and the holiday it is associated with. After verifying that the candy cane is associated with Christmas, explain that the picture on the chalkboard is a *symbol*—a simple picture that stands for an idea or object. Then tell students that there are various symbols associated with holidays and religions throughout the world.

Steps:

1. Explain to students that people all over the world celebrate many different types of holidays. Share with students the different kinds of holidays: religious holidays (e.g., Christmas), calendar holidays (e.g., New Year's Day), folklore-related holidays (e.g., Halloween), and national holidays (e.g., Fourth of July).

2. Give each student a copy of page 49. For each symbol card, name the holiday that the symbol represents. Also share a brief description of the holiday. (See the Background Information on page 47 for descriptions of some of the holidays.) Then challenge students to brainstorm additional symbols that are associated with any holiday they are already familiar with.

3. Direct students to cut out the symbol cards. Have each child glue the cards onto her gameboard in random order. While students are programming their gameboards, distribute the game markers.

4. Announce the game to be played, such as three in a vertical row, four corners, or five in a horizontal row. To play, take a card and announce the name of the holiday associated with the symbol on the card. Have each student find the corresponding symbol on her gameboard, and direct her to cover the space with a game marker. The first student to cover the gameboard spaces needed to win announces "Hooray for holidays!" Then she verifies her win by naming the holiday associated with each symbol that she covered. To begin a new game, ask students to clear their gameboards. Place the cards back in the container, and invite the winner of the previous game to be the caller, if desired.

Name ____________________ *Recognizing symbols of different holidays*

Hooray For Holidays!

Cut.
Glue
Follow your teacher's directions.

How To Extend The Lesson:

- This large-group game helps youngsters learn about holiday symbols. For every two students, program an index card with a different holiday symbol; then, for each symbol card, label another index card with the name of the corresponding holiday name. To play, randomly distribute both sets of cards. Each student reads his card and searches for the classmate who has the matching card. When two students discover that their cards match, they sit down. After each student has found his match, collect and shuffle the cards; then play the game again!

- Broaden students' knowledge of other cultures by sharing information on holidays such as Bastille Day, Boxing Day, Divali, Midsummer's Day, Ramadan, Sukkot, and Yom Kippur. *Why Do We Celebrate That?* by Jane Wilcox (Franklin Watts, Inc.; 1996) is a good choice. This information-packed resource reveals many interesting facts about holidays and celebrations throughout the world.

- This class book is the perfect place for students to show off their knowledge of holiday symbols. Assign a holiday symbol to each student (or student pair). Have each student draw and color a picture of her symbol on a sheet of white paper. Next have her trim around the symbol and glue it to the top of a sheet of colorful construction paper. Below the illustration, have her write the name of the holiday the symbol represents. Bind the completed pages between decorated construction-paper covers and title the book "Here's To Holiday Symbols!"

Families Around The World

This first-class multicultural lesson is just the ticket for helping students develop an awareness and respect for the diversity of families around the world.

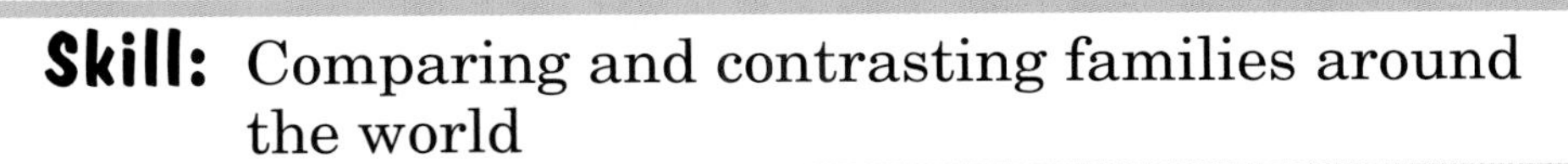

Skill: Comparing and contrasting families around the world

Estimated Lesson Time: 30 minutes

Teacher Preparation:

1. Duplicate page 53 for each student.
2. Cut paper for each child. (See the list below.)

Materials:

1 copy of page 53 per student
six 6" x 9" sheets of blank paper
two 6" x 9" sheets of colorful construction paper
scissors
glue
crayons
stapler

Background Information:

Family life differs around the world. Families can contain any number of people, from one parent and a child to large groups of people related by birth or marriage. Although the cultural traditions of families are different, all families provide food, clothing, and shelter to their members.

Introducing The Lesson:

Describe your family to students, being sure to share favorite family meals, activities, and other things that make your family unique. Next encourage students to talk about their families. Then lead students in a discussion about the similarities and differences among their families.

Steps:

1. Share with students the Background Information on page 51. Then introduce students to family life in five different countries with this booklet activity. Give each child glue, scissors, crayons, six sheets of blank paper, and a copy of page 53. To begin, announce one of the five countries listed below and read aloud the provided information. Then have each child color the corresponding picture on page 53, cut it out, glue it to a blank sheet of paper, and write a sentence or two about it. Continue in this same manner for each country. On the remaining sheet of blank paper, have the child draw a picture of her family and write a short description of her family life.

2. To create a booklet, a child binds the pages between two 6" x 9" sheets of construction paper. Then she titles the cover "Families Around The World," and personalizes it as desired. Encourage students to take their resulting photo albums home to share with their families.

Family Facts

Mexico—Families are usually large. Often the father works and the mother stays at home. Grandparents and other relatives sometimes live in the home too. The family usually eats lunch together and then rests. Tortillas, beans, and rice are major Mexican foods.

Brazil—Since many men have jobs as truckers and are not home during the week, families live close to their relatives who can help out. In poorer families the children sometimes work. Soccer is a favorite sport. Lunch is the most important meal of the day. On Saturdays, most people eat *feijoada,* which is a meal that combines dried and smoked meats with black beans.

France—Children often stay up late at night talking over dinner, reading, or watching television. Cycling is a popular family activity. Families try to eat all their meals together, which sometimes last more than two hours. Escargots (hot snails with garlic butter), crêpes, and pâté are popular French foods.

Ghana—In this West African country, village life is very different from city life. Villagers still have to fetch their own water and grow their own food. The modern cities though have many of the services that the United States has. A popular food is *banku,* which is made from corn dough and a plant root. Yams, rice, fish, and groundnuts are also popular foods.

China—Due to problems with overcrowding, the government has required couples living in cities to have just one child. Grandparents usually take care of the children because both parents often work six days a week. At mealtime each person has a bowl of rice, and he uses chopsticks to take food from the main dishes. Rice, dumplings, meat or fish, and vegetables are popular foods. Bowling is a popular activity.

Photograph Cards

Use with Step 1 on page 52.

A family from Mexico

Completed Project

A family from Brazil

A family from France

A family from China

A family from Ghana

How To Extend The Lesson:

- This booklet project is perfect for reviewing the similarities and differences of family life between two countries. To make the booklet, a child folds a 9" x 12" sheet of drawing paper in half (to 6" x 9") and makes a cut in the top layer to create two same-size flaps. Next she labels a flap for each country. On each flap, she draws and colors a scene illustrating family life in this country. Under each flap, the student writes a brief description of the family life in that country.

- Celebrate the diversity of family cultures throughout the world with this tasty idea. Over the course of a few weeks, ask each parent to prepare a favorite recipe that has cultural significance to her family origin. Also ask the parent to write the recipe and the country it originated from on a sheet of paper. Compile the recipes into a class cookbook; then duplicate student copies. What a delicious keepsake for students to share with their families.

- Share desired sections of *Children Just Like Me* by Susan Elizabeth Copsey, Barnabas Kindersley, and Harry Belafonte (Dorling Kindersley Publishing, Inc.; 1995) with students. This informative book takes a look at homes, schools, family life, and cultures of children around the world. After sharing information about a particular area of the world, challenge students to compare family life in the United States to family life in this area. To do this, post a chart like the one shown. Then write the student-generated comparisons in the appropriate areas on the chart. Repeat this process for each country that you read about from the book.

	France	United States
homes		
schools		
foods		
clothing		
popular activities		

A Diversity Of Dwellings

There's no place like home for learning. So move right into this lesson on comparing and contrasting homes around the world.

Skill: Comparing and contrasting homes from other cultures

Estimated Lesson Time: 45 minutes

Teacher Preparation:
Duplicate page 57 for each student.

Materials:
1 copy of page 57 per student
scissors
globe or world map

Background Information:

Shelters or homes can be made of many different materials. People build shelters or homes from materials that are available where they live. Homes can be made from brick, concrete, wood, stone, animal skins, and other materials. For example, in countries where there are many forests, most houses would be built with wood as the main building material.

The climate of an area also affects the type of shelter. For example, in wet climates like Thailand, people often build houses on poles, or *stilts,* so their homes do not flood. In mountain areas, some people build homes right into the side of a mountain to protect them from the strong winds.

In some places, the type of home depends on the amount of available land. For example, some cities have so many people there isn't enough land for everyone to build a house. In these cities, many people live in apartment buildings.

Introducing The Lesson:

Ask a student volunteer to describe what her home looks like. Encourage her to include its color and what material it was built with. Next ask a few other students to describe their homes. Lead students to realize that although some people have similar homes, there are also differences between them. Then tell students that some homes in other parts of the world are even more different and that they will be learning about some of those homes today.

Steps:

1. Explain to students the three reasons the types of homes or shelters around the world differ. (See the Background Information on page 55). Be sure to remind students that people who live in the same part of the world can live in different kinds of homes and people who live in different parts of the world can live in the same kinds of homes.

2. Distribute a copy of page 57 to each student. For each game card, share the information shown below about the home. Also point out on a globe or map the area of the world where the home is located.
   - **apartment building in Hong Kong—**People live in groups of rooms called apartments. Usually there are several apartments on each floor and several floors in each building.
   - **tent in Saudi Arabia—**People who need to move often to find water and food for animals sometimes live in tents since they are easy to move.
   - **chalet in Switzerland—**This home is built of wood. Almost everything inside the home is made of wood too. The snow on the roof helps to keep heat in.
   - **floating home in Vietnam—**Some people live in floating homes because the cities are too crowded. Others live on the water because of what they do for a living (e.g., catch fish).
   - **home on stilts in New Guinea—**This home sits on stilts so it won't flood during the rainy season.
   - **mountain home in Bolivia—**Mountain areas are very windy and cold; therefore the houses must be sturdy. This home is made of stone.
   - **arctic home in northern Canada—**This home is above the ground because the ground is frozen all year long. If the home was on the ground, the heat from the floor would thaw the frozen soil and the house would sink.
   - **hut in Africa—**Huts can be made of mud, clay, stones, grass, bark, or branches. Few huts have electricity or running water. A grass hut is the coolest type of home.
   - **adobe home in Mexico—**This home is made of *adobe,* blocks of clay and straw baked dry in the sun. Thick adobe walls help keep out the heat.

3. Have students cut out their game cards. Then pair students and share with them the provided playing instructions for the memory-style card game.

Directions:
- Shuffle both sets of cards together and arrange them facedown on a playing surface. Determine which player will take his turn first.
- The first player turns over two cards. If two identical cards are revealed, the player names the type of home shown and its location (optional). Then he keeps the cards and turns over two more. If the two cards turned over do not match as described above, the player turns them facedown again, and his turn is over.
- The second player takes his turn in a similar manner.
- Play continues in this manner until all of the cards are matched.
- The child with the most cards wins the game.

Use with Steps 2 and 3 on page 56.

OUR NEIGHBORS

How To Extend The Lesson:

- Divide the class into small groups and assign each group a different climate, such as rainy and warm, windy and snowy, or hot and dry. Then challenge each group to work together to create a drawing of a house that would be suitable for the assigned climate. After the groups have completed their work, ask one member from each group to share its drawing and explain the design.

- Build time into your schedule to share these books about houses around the world.
  — *Houses And Homes* by Carol Bowyer (EDC Publications, 1978)
  — *Houses* by Claude Delafosse (Scholastic Inc., 1998)
  — *Homes Around The World* (Crabtree Publishing Company, 1994)

- Share *The Dream House* by Pirkko Vainio (North-South Books Inc., 1997) with your youngsters. In this delightful book, a man builds his dream house on an island. After a bad storm, the house ends up as a covered bridge to the mainland, which suits the builder just fine! After an oral reading, invite your youngsters to design their own dream homes. To do this, each child designs his home on drawing paper and then lists on an index card what materials the home would be made of. Mount each student's completed design beside his index card on a bulletin board titled "A Parade Of Homes!"

A Holiday Timeline

This timely holiday card game provides plenty of practice with timelines!

Skill: Sequencing major U.S. holidays using timelines

Estimated Lesson Time: 45 minutes

Teacher Preparation:

1. Duplicate page 61 for each student plus one extra.
2. Cut out one copy of the cards.
3. Cut a three-foot length of yarn for each student.
4. From bulletin-board paper, cut a 36-inch strip per student.

Materials:

1 copy of page 61 per student plus one extra
one 3-foot length of yarn per student
one 5" x 36" paper strip per student
tape
glue
scissors
crayons

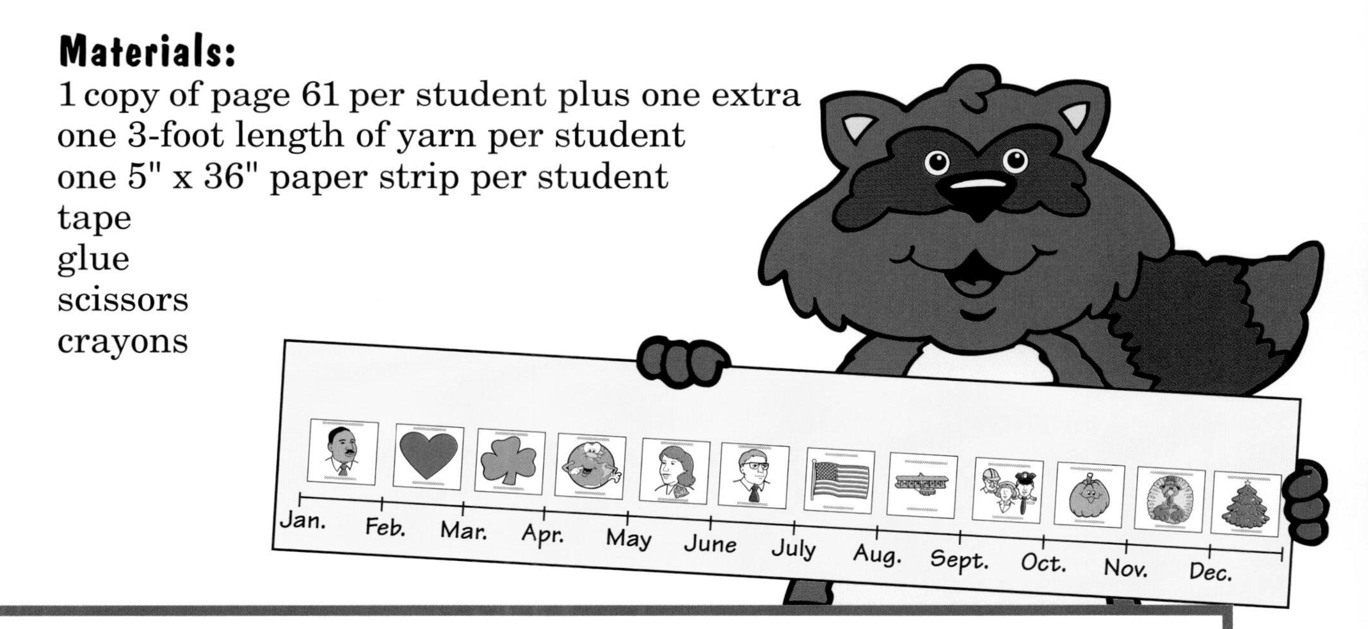

Background Information:
A timeline is a line that shows the events of a time period in the order in which they happened. Reading timelines can help you understand when things happened, in what order they happened, and how much time passed between events. A timeline is read from left to right, like a sentence. The events on the left of the timeline happened the earliest. The events that happened later are on the right. A timeline can show the events in any time period, such as 1,000 years or an hour.

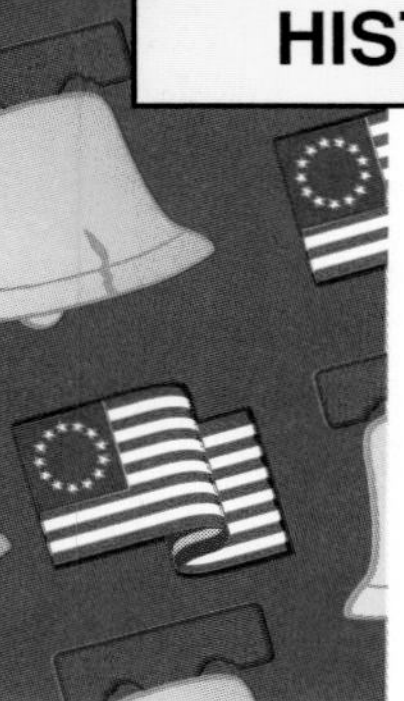

HISTORY

Introducing The Lesson:

Ask students to name a variety of holidays. Write their responses on the chalkboard in random order. Next tell students that you would like to arrange the holidays in the order they occur during the year. Ask students for suggestions on how to do this. Then explain that a timeline is one way to show the chronological order of the holidays.

Steps:

1. Share the Background Information about timelines on page 59.

2. On the chalkboard, draw a timeline beginning with January and ending with December. (See the illustration on page 59.) Then randomly display one of the holiday cards. Enlist students' help in determining where to place the card on the timeline. Use tape to attach the card to the appropriate spot on the timeline. Continue in this manner for each remaining card.

3. Distribute a copy of page 61 to each student. Have him cut out the holiday cards. Then pair students and share with them the playing instructions (shown below) for the card game Holiday Timeline.

4. When game time is over, have each twosome sort their cards so that each player has one of each card. Then give each child a 5" x 36" paper strip, a three-foot length of yarn, crayons, and glue. Have each child glue his yarn on the paper strip in a horizontal line to represent a timeline. While the yarn is drying, have him color the holiday cards; then have him glue the cards in chronological order to the yarn.

Directions for playing Holiday Timeline:

- The game is for two players and is played like the card game War.
- One player shuffles the two sets of cards together. Then the other player evenly deals out all the cards keeping them facedown.
- Both players turn over their top cards at the same time. Each player states the holiday represented on his card.
- The player whose holiday is closest to the beginning of the timeline shown on the chalkboard wins the round. He then puts his partner's card and his card facedown at the bottom of his card stack.
- If both players turn over the same card, each player turns over a second card to determine the winner of the round.
- Play continues in this manner until one player has all the cards or until game time is over.

Use with Steps 2, 3, and 4 on page 60.

Martin Luther King Jr. Day January	Valentine's Day February	St. Patrick's Day March
Earth Day April	Mother's Day May	Father's Day June
Fourth Of July July	National Aviation Day August	Labor Day September
Halloween October	Thanksgiving November	Christmas December

How To Extend The Lesson:

- Give each student a copy of page 61 and have her cut out her cards. Pair the students and give each pair a three-foot length of yarn. Each twosome places its yarn in a horizontal line to represent a timeline that starts at January. Then the pair stacks its combined holiday cards facedown. In turn, each child draws a holiday card and places it in sequential order on the timeline. If a student draws a card with a holiday that has already been played, she places the card on top of its duplicate. Students continue in this manner until all the cards are played.

- Enlist your students' help in making a human timeline. Place a long strip of masking tape on the floor to depict a timeline. Ask 12 volunteers to come to the front of the classroom. Randomly give each volunteer an enlarged holiday card (page 61) and have him hold it with the writing facing outward. Then enlist the help of the remaining students to sequence the students holding the holiday cards in chronological order beginning with January. Repeat the activity until each child has had a turn holding a card.

- Once students have a good understanding of sequencing holidays on a timeline, have them try sequencing their birthdays. On a long length of bulletin-board paper that is approximately one foot wide, draw a line the length of the paper as shown. Have your students stand and organize themselves chronologically (starting with January) according to their birthdays. Once in order, have each child write his name and date of birth on the timeline. Display the completed birthday timeline in a prominent classroom location.

OUR CLASSROOM BIRTHDAY TIMELINE

Jan.	Feb.	Mar.	Apr.	May	June	July	Aug.	Sept.	Oct.	Nov.	Dec.
3-Laura	5-Ben	7-Peter	7-Billy	10-Sharon	11-Cathy	9-Tia	15-David	12-Jennifer	3-Jason	16-Kate	6-Jay
12-Seth	21-Molly		19-Jessie	13-Josh	20-Donna			13-Chris	10-Hannah	19-Liza	
					30-Kevin					25-Daniel	

Time For School!

Ring the bell and gather students for this lesson about schools from long ago!

Skill: Comparing and contrasting schools of today with those from the past

Estimated Lesson Time: 40 minutes

Teacher Preparation:

1. Duplicate page 65 and the picture cards on page 66 for each student.
2. Label a chart with the headings and categories shown on page 64.

Materials:

1 copy of page 65 per student
1 copy of the picture cards on page 66 per student
chart paper
scissors
glue
crayons

Background Information:

- **Supplies:** The early schools had only two books: the Bible and a primer that contained the alphabet, spelling words, numbers, and poems. Some children wrote in *copybooks,* or booklets of blank paper. Students who couldn't afford copybooks wrote on *slates* (similar to small blackboards).
- **Schoolhouse:** Most country schools were one-room buildings with only one or two windows to let in light. A fireplace or woodstove was used for heat. One teacher taught all the children in the school. Children sat on simple benches.
- **Getting To School:** The school was usually a long way from home. Most students walked to school, some with bare feet. A few children had horses they could ride to get there.
- **Lessons:** Since schoolbooks and paper were scarce, students recited passages from memory and the teacher corrected any mistakes. They also practiced their penmanship a lot.
- **Running The School:** Families gave wood to the school for the woodstove. Children took turns fetching fresh drinking water.
- **Punishment:** Some children who misbehaved had to wear a dunce cap or a sign. Others had to write lines over and over or balance on a block of wood in a corner of the classroom.
- **Lunch:** Students carried lunch baskets or tin pails. Lunch often included homemade bread with jam and donuts or pie.

Introducing The Lesson:

Post the chart in a prominent area. Ask students to name any supplies that they use at school. Write students' responses under the heading "Schools Of Today" and beside the category "supplies." Next ask students to imagine what school would be like if they didn't have many of these supplies. Then share the Background Information (page 63) about supplies in schools of long ago.

	Schools Of The Past	*Schools Of Today*
supplies	slates, primers, copybooks, rulers	paper, crayons, markers, notebooks, paint, scissors, glue, stapler, computers, rulers
schoolhouse		
getting to school		
lessons		
running the school		
punishment		
lunch		

Steps:

1. Announce the second category shown on the chart ("schoolhouse"). Ask students to describe what their school looks like. Write their responses in the appropriate location on the chart. Then share the Background Information on page 63 about schoolhouses from long ago. Record this information on the chart.

2. Continue in this same manner for the remaining categories on the chart.

3. Distribute scissors, crayons, glue, a copy of page 65, and a copy of the picture cards to each student. Explain to students that two writing surfaces are shown—one used in schools from long ago (slate) and one used in today's schools (notebook). Next instruct each child to color and cut out the picture cards. Then, for each card, have her decide if the picture shown is something from school days of long ago or today. Then have her glue the cards on the corresponding writing surface.

4. Challenge students to complete the Bonus Box activity.

Name ______________________ *Comparing and contrasting schools of today with those of the past*

Time For School

Follow your teacher's directions.

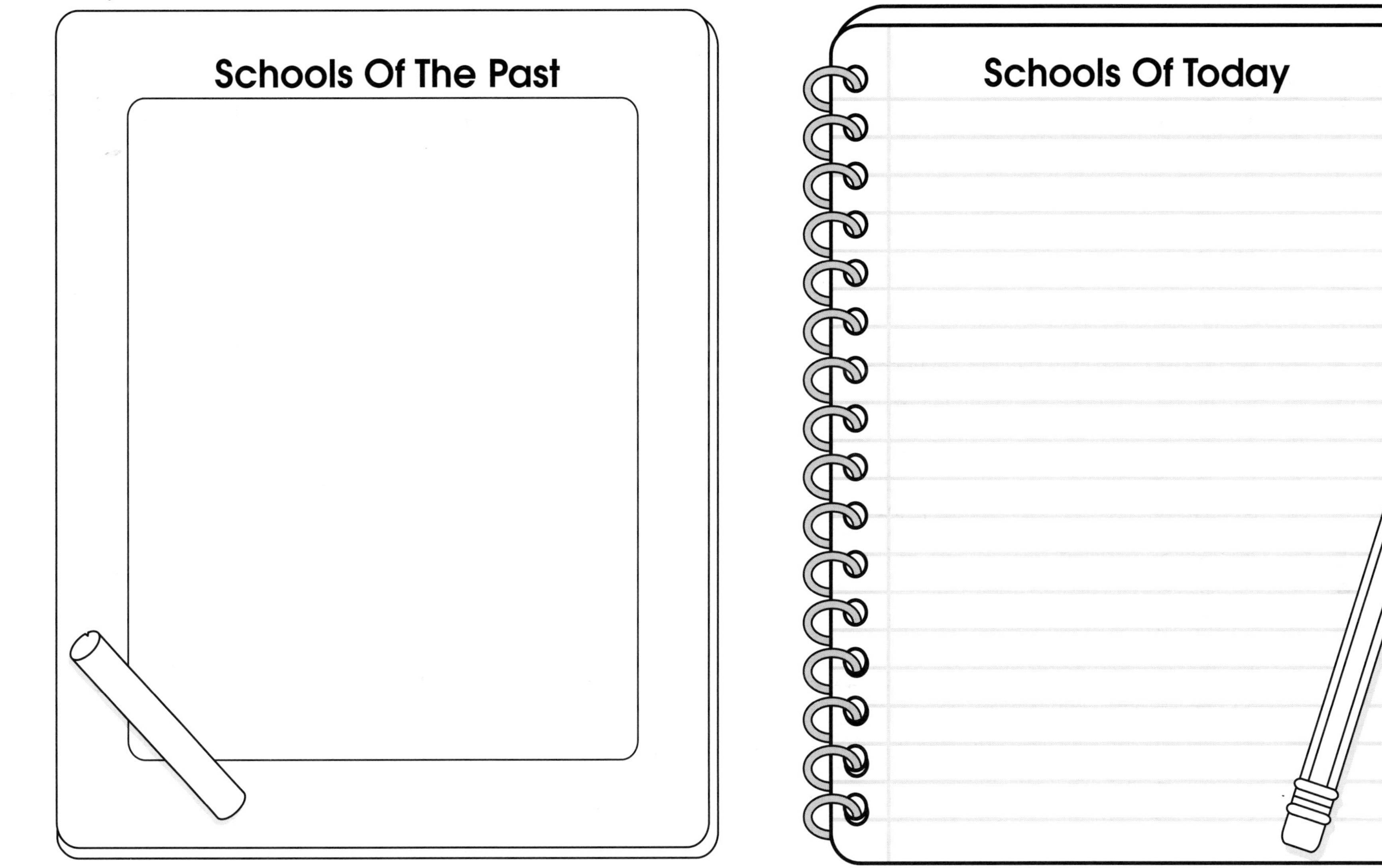

Bonus Box: Would you have liked going to school in earlier times? Why or why not? Write your answer on the back of this sheet.

How To Extend The Lesson:

- Schoolchildren of long ago dipped the tips of feathers into ink bottles and then practiced their handwriting. Have your young writers practice their handwriting with similar writing instruments. Pour black tempera paint in a container and add a drop or two of water; then stir. Place the paint, feathers, and a supply of paper at a writing center. Have each student visit the center and try her hand at practicing penmanship with a quill pen and ink.

- At the beginning of each school day, students "made their manners" to their teacher. Boys bowed and girls curtsied. Students were also told to make their manners to any adults they met. Lead students to realize that although they do not bow or curtsy to adults, they still make their manners in other ways, such as addressing adults as sir or ma'am, saying thank you and please, and being respectful. Then have each child create a card for his parents telling them how he makes his manners toward them.

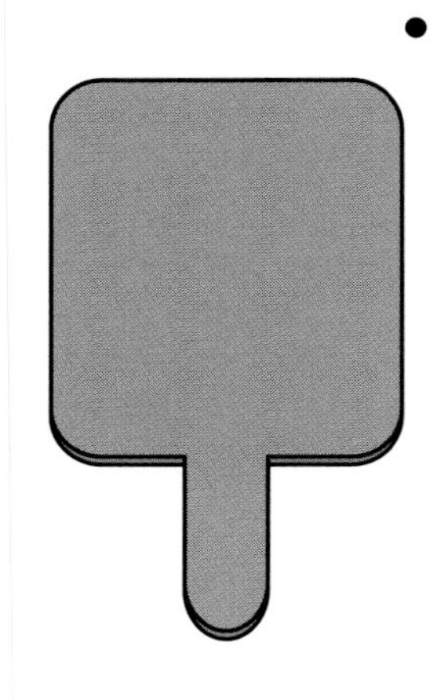

- In the 1770s some students used *hornbooks,* wooden paddles with lesson sheets attached to them. A thin, transparent piece of horn protected the lesson sheet since paper was so expensive. Have students create their own hornbooks. To do this, a student traces a hornbook template (see the illustration) onto tagboard. She cuts out the pattern and punches a hole in the handle; then she threads a length of yarn through the hole and ties the yarn's ends so the yarn will fit loosely around her wrist. Next give each student a list of math facts or spelling words that you would like her to learn. Have her cover the lesson sheet with a piece of laminating film of the same size and then attach the pages to her hornbook with two brads.

Picture Cards

Use with Step 3 on page 64.

Historical Heroes

Introduce your students to a variety of famous people with this pictorial lesson.

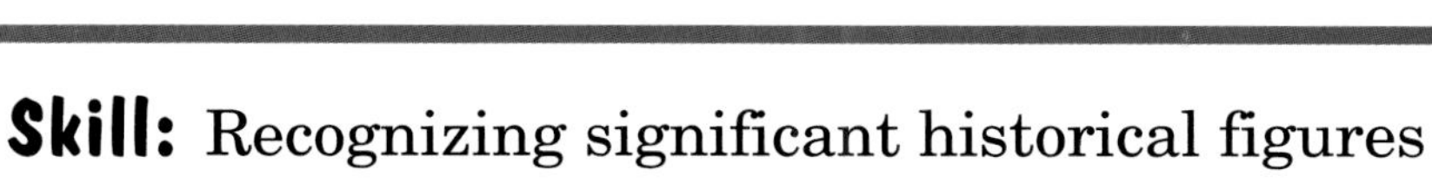

Skill: Recognizing significant historical figures

Estimated Lesson Time: 30 minutes

Teacher Preparation:

1. Duplicate page 69 for each student.
2. Cut two 2 1/2" x 3 1/2" pieces of colorful construction paper for each student.

Materials:

1 copy of page 69 per student
two 2 1/2" x 3 1/2" pieces of colorful construction paper per student
yarn
glue
hole puncher
crayons
scissors

Background Information:

- **Martin Luther King Jr.** was the main leader of the civil rights movement in the United States. He gave speeches to help people understand that all people are important, no matter what color they are.
- **George Washington** led the army that won American independence from Great Britain in the Revolutionary War. He helped write the United States Constitution, and he was elected the first president of the United States.
- **Abraham Lincoln,** the 16th president of the United States, led the United States during the Civil War and helped to end slavery.
- **Harriet Tubman,** as a leader of the Underground Railroad, helped hundreds of slaves escape to freedom.
- **Helen Keller,** who rose above her disabilities of being blind and deaf, wrote books and gave speeches to inspire the blind and deaf and to educate the public about the handicapped.
- **Neil Armstrong,** an astronaut, was the first person to walk on the moon. He landed on the moon on July 20, 1969.

Introducing The Lesson:

Tell students you have a brainteaser for them. Then ask students to name something that can be found on a dollar bill, a stamp, and a baseball card. After students have made several guesses, explain that the faces of famous people are found on these items. Then tell students that as they learn about several famous people from the past, they will make a historical hero card for each person.

Steps:

1. Distribute a copy of page 69 to each student. For each historical hero card, share information about the person. (See the Background Information on page 67.)

2. Read aloud the descriptions at the bottom of the reproducible. Next have each student cut out the descriptions and glue each description to its corresponding card. Then have each student color the pictures and then cut out the completed cards.

3. Have each student compile her cards into a historical hero booklet. To do this, give each child two 2 1/2" x 3 1/2" pieces of colorful construction paper. Instruct her to stack her cards between the construction-paper pieces. Hole-punch the papers near the middle of the left margin; then thread a length of yarn through the holes and securely tie the yarn ends. Finally, have her title the resulting booklet "Historical Heroes" and decorate the front cover as desired.

4. Encourage students to take their historical heroes booklets home to share with their families.

Name ______________________________

Historical Figures

Follow your teacher's directions.

Martin Luther King Jr.	George Washington	Abraham Lincoln
Harriet Tubman	**Helen Keller**	**Neil Armstrong**

first president of the United States	gave speeches to inspire the blind and the deaf	a leader of the Underground Railroad
first person to walk on the moon	a leader of the civil rights movement	16th president of the United States

How To Extend The Lesson:

- This whole-class project results in a historical hero quilt! To begin, have each child choose a historical figure he has enjoyed learning about. Then have him write a short description of this person's accomplishments on a seven-inch square of white paper. If desired, have him also draw a picture of the person on the square. Next have him center the square atop a nine-inch construction-paper square and glue it in place. Mount the completed quilt patches on a length of bulletin-board paper. Use a marker to draw "stitches" around each project. Display the quilt and a title such as "A Quilt Of Historical Heroes" on a classroom wall!

- Have students make famous people portraits to grace the walls of their classroom. In advance, gather information and pictures of several historical figures that students are interested in. (See the list below for suggestions.) Share the information about these people with students. To create a portrait, a student chooses a person and draws a picture of him or her on a large oval cutout. Next she labels a yellow rectangle with the person's name and a short description of his or her accomplishment. The student mounts the resulting brass plate and the portrait on a large sheet of colorful construction paper. If desired, add a paper frame around each child's project before mounting them in the hallway!

More Historical Heroes

Clara Barton—nurse and founder of the American Red Cross
George Washington Carver—teacher and botanist who created many new uses for soybeans, sweet potatoes, and peanuts
Amelia Earhart—first woman to fly across the Atlantic Ocean alone
Jackie Robinson—first Black American player in major league baseball
Betsy Ross—maker of the first American flag, according to legend
Garrett Morgan—invented the three-way traffic stoplight
Squanto—Pawtuxet Indian leader who befriended the Pilgrims of Plymouth Colony and taught them how to plant corn

Hot On The Trail!

Get your youngsters on the right track with wants and needs using this gameboard activity.

Skill: Distinguishing between wants and needs

Estimated Lesson Time: 45 minutes

Teacher Preparation:
Duplicate page 73 for each student pair.

Materials:
1 copy of page 73 per student pair
1 sheet of drawing paper per student
1 penny per student pair
1 game marker per student (different-colored Unifix® cubes or counters)
crayons

Background Information:
- People must have certain things, called *needs,* to live. Food, shelter, clothing, love, and safety are our basic needs.
- *Wants* are things a person desires or wishes for but does not have to have for survival or well-being.
- People have unlimited wants.

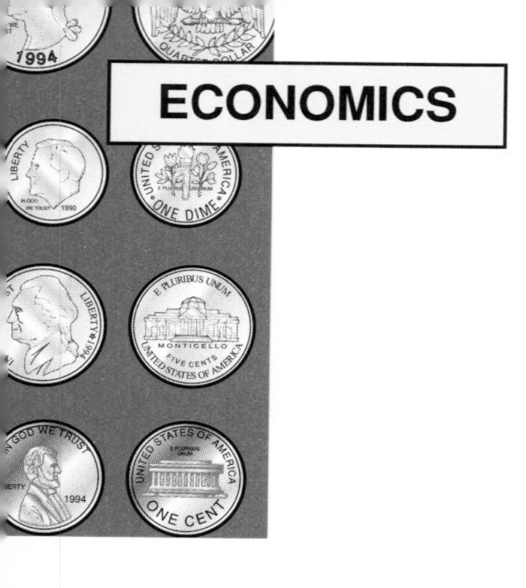

Introducing The Lesson:

Give each child a sheet of drawing paper and have her quickly draw the outline of her home in the middle of the paper. After students have completed their drawings, tell them that they are going to use their drawings to help learn about wants and needs.

Steps:

1. Use the Background Information on page 71 to review with students the terms *wants* and *needs*. List the basic needs on the chalkboard along with examples of several wants.

2. Refer students to the outlines of their homes. Ask them whether their homes are a want or a need. Have each child label her home as a need. Next have each student draw and/or list the other needs inside her home outline. Then, around her house, have her draw pictures of five items she or her family owns that are wants. Provide time for students to share their work.

3. Pair students and distribute page 73, one penny, and two game markers to each student pair.

4. Share with students the following directions for playing the wants and needs game:
   - Students place their markers on START.
   - A student flips the coin and moves:
     Heads = 1 space
     Tails = 2 spaces
   - If there are directions written on the space, the student follows the directions. If there is a picture on the space, she must correctly identify the picture as a want or a need.
     —If the answer is approved by her partner, she may stay.
     —If the answer is not approved, she returns to her original space.
   - The first player to reach FINISH wins.

Hot On The Trail!

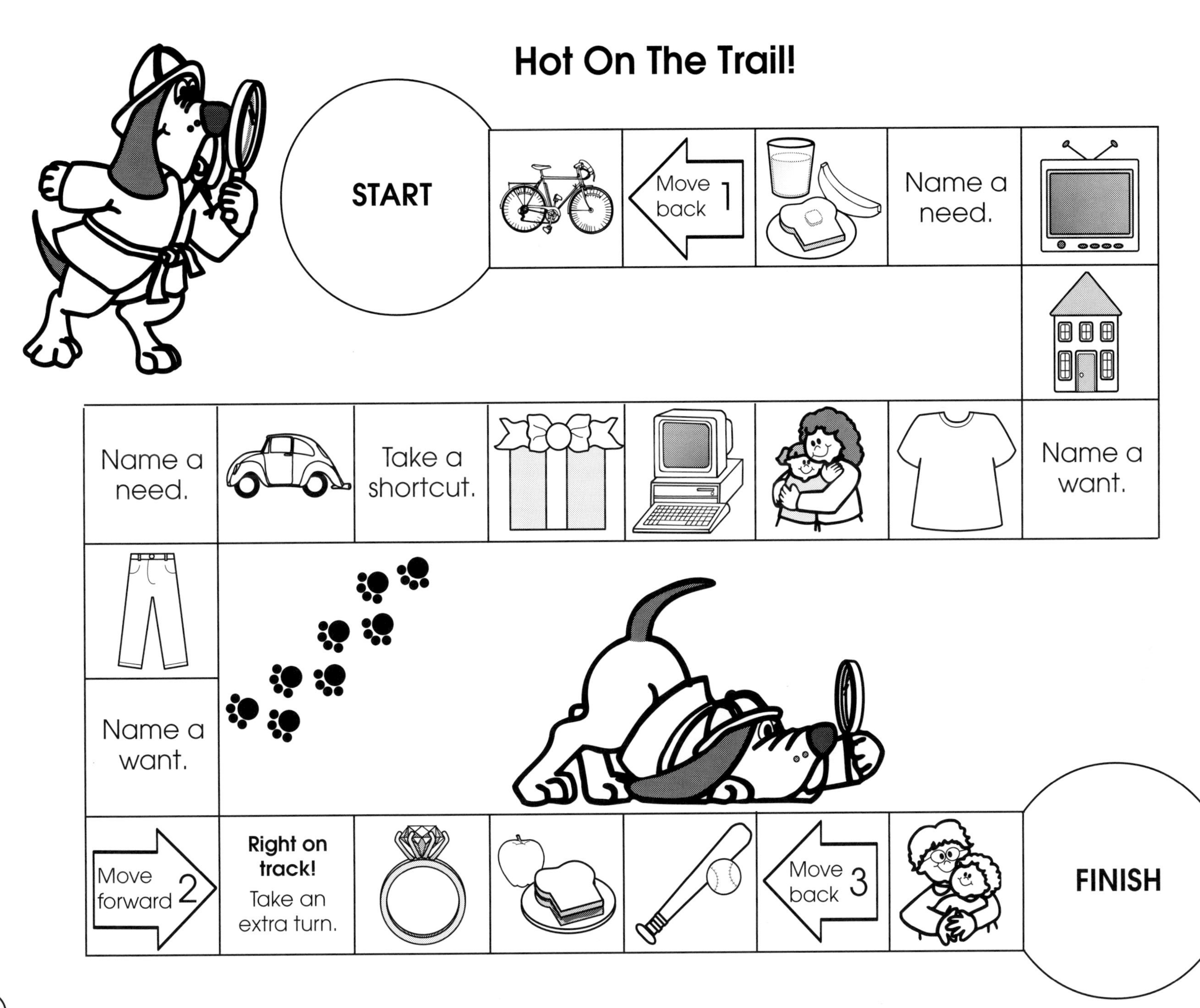

How To Extend The Lesson:

- Students create wants and needs body posters with this activity. Have each child lie down on a piece of bulletin-board paper slightly larger than her body. Draw the outline of each child's body; then have the child add facial features. Next instruct students to cut out pictures from magazines (or draw pictures) of their wants and needs and glue them to their outlines. Display the completed projects in the hallway for all to see!

- Divide students into small groups to brainstorm lists for the following topics:
  —needs of a baby
  —wants of their families
  —wants that do not cost money

- Provide students with five minutes to make lists of all their wants. Next read aloud *The Berenstain Bears Get The Gimmies* by Jan and Stan Berenstain (Random House, Inc.; 1988). After sharing the book, discuss with students the concept of unlimited wants. Then have each child review his list and decide on the three most important wants on his list. Invite each student to share his three wants with the class.

- Enlist students' help in making a list of wants and needs for the classroom. Record students' responses on chart paper. Then challenge students to decide which items are the most important and explain why.

In The Classroom	
Wants	**Needs**
• new computer	• everyone to care for each other
• new crayons	• everyone to be kind
• more books	• lunch and snack
• curtains for the windows	
• a beanbag chair	
• carpet	
• an art easel	

Just Not Enough!

There will be no shortage of learning with this lesson about shortages of school-related items!

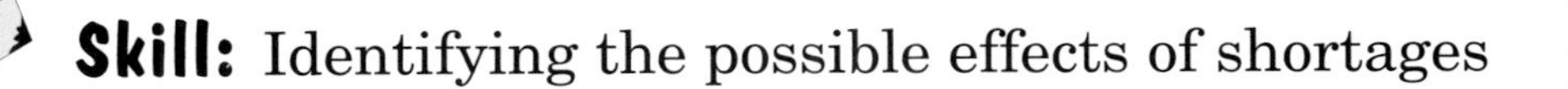

Skill: Identifying the possible effects of shortages

Estimated Lesson Time: 30 minutes

Teacher Preparation:

1. Duplicate page 77 for each student.
2. Duplicate the picture cards on page 78 for each student.

Materials:

1 copy of page 77 per student
1 copy of the picture cards on page 78 per student
2 sheets of blank paper per small group
2 markers per small group
crayons
scissors
glue

Background Information:

A *shortage* occurs when the demand for something is larger than the supply. When there is a shortage of an item, the item's value increases until the supply increases or until the demand decreases (both of which would reduce the shortage). There is never a shortage of items that people do not want.

Introducing The Lesson:

Divide students into groups of four or five and ask each group to sit in a circle. Place two pieces of paper and two markers in the center of each circle. Next ask each student to use a marker to write her name on a sheet of the provided paper. As students begin to realize there are not enough supplies, direct students to stop what they are doing. Then ask them to describe the problem (a *shortage* of supplies) and talk about the effects of this problem (not everyone can complete the assignment).

Steps:

1. Share the Background Information on page 75. Explain to students that there is a shortage of paper for the assignment. Then distribute paper to each student who does not already have a sheet. Have students share the markers to complete the assignment. After students have completed writing their names, guide students to understand that they were able to overcome the shortage of the paper but not the markers.

2. Invite students to share other times that they experienced shortages, such as when a popular toy or a favorite ice-cream flavor was sold out at the store. Also ask that they tell the effects of these shortages.

3. Distribute a copy of page 77 and the picture cards on page 78 to each student. Have each child color three pictures, cut them out, and glue each one to a blank box on page 77. For each picture, ask students to imagine that there is a shortage of the school item. Then have them write about the possible effects of this shortage.

4. Challenge students to complete the Bonus Box activity.

5. Set aside time for students to share their work with each other.

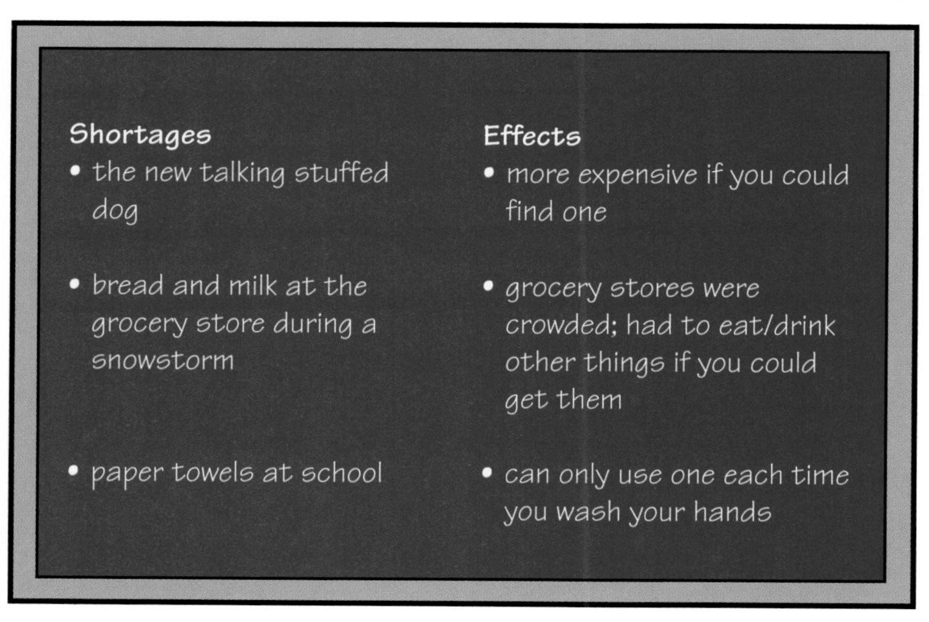

Name ______________________ *Identifying the possible effects of shortages*

Just Not Enough!

Follow your teacher's directions.

1. ______________________

2. ______________________

3. ______________________

Bonus Box: Think of an item in your home. Draw a picture of it on the back of this sheet. Write a sentence to tell what it might be like if there was a shortage of this item.

How To Extend The Lesson:

- Further demonstrate the concept of a shortage by inviting students to play several rounds of musical chairs. It won't take long to see that a shortage of chairs leads to fewer people playing the game!

- Remind students that there can be shortages of our natural resources. Discuss with students the importance of keeping the water, air, and all living things in abundant supply. Also ask students to talk about the possible effects of shortages in our natural resources. Then have students imagine there is a water shortage. Place students in small groups and assign a recorder in each one. Then challenge each group to create tips for conserving water as the recorder lists them on paper. After a designated amount of time, ask each group to share its tips. For added fun, ask each group to make a poster showcasing its conservation tips. Post the completed posters around the school to encourage others to conserve!

- These individual journals are the perfect place for students to record what-ifs about shortages. To make a journal for each child, staple a supply of writing paper between two construction-paper covers of equal size. Have each child personalize a journal and store it in her desk. Each day, post a question such as "What if there were a shortage of chocolate?" or "What if there were a shortage of school buses?" Then have each child write about the possible effects of this shortage in her journal.

Picture Cards

Use with Step 3 on page 76.

Shopping For Goods And Services

Learning about goods and services is in the bag with this booklet-making lesson!

Skill: Distinguishing between goods and services

Estimated Lesson Time: 40 minutes

Teacher Preparation:

1. Duplicate page 81 for each student.
2. Draw a line to divide a large sheet of chart paper in half. Label one side of the chart "Goods" and the other side "Services."
3. Place a good such as a snack item or school supply in a grocery bag.

Materials:

1 copy of page 81 per student
labeled sheet of chart paper
grocery bag containing a good
crayons
scissors
glue
stapler

Background Information:

People use goods and services each day. *Goods* are items that people make (such as televisions) or grow (such as apples). *Services* are jobs that people pay others to do because they cannot or do not want to do the jobs themselves. Dental checkups and haircuts are examples of services.

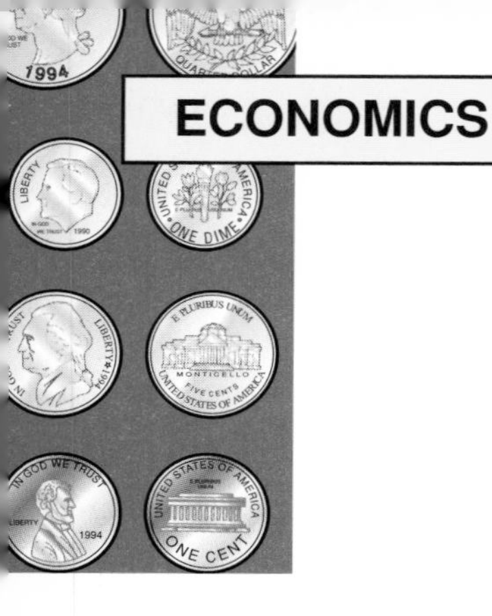

Introducing The Lesson:

Show students the shopping bag as you tell them that you ran two errands yesterday. Remove the item from the bag and tell students where you purchased it. Then tell students you also took your car in to be repaired. Ask students why you don't have anything in the bag to show that you had your car repaired. Lead students to understand that you didn't purchase an item from the car mechanic, rather the mechanic performed a *service* on the car.

Steps:

1. Explain to students that the item (from the bag) is a *good* and the car repair you had done is a *service*. Then share the Background Information on page 79.

2. Post the labeled chart in a prominent classroom location. Write the name of the item from the bag under the column labeled "Goods" on the chart. Then write "car repair" under the column labeled "Services." Next challenge students to name additional goods and services. Write each response in the appropriate column.

3. Distribute a copy of page 81 to each student. Have each child write his name on the provided line. Next have him color and cut out the boxes at the bottom of the page. In turn, read each sentence describing a community worker and have students glue the corresponding picture on the booklet page. Next have them mark a check in the corresponding box to state whether the worker provides a good or a service.

4. After each student completes the booklet pages, have him cut out the pages on the bold lines. Then have him stack the booklet pages behind the cover and staple along the left-hand margin. Encourage students to take their mini books home to share with their families.

Goods	Services
apple	car repair
phone	hairstyling
car	dental checkup
book	painting
toy	collecting garbage

Use with Steps 3 and 4 on page 80.

My Goods And Services Mini Book by ______________ Name	I help children learn. I provide a ☐ good ☐ service
I make clothes. I provide a ☐ good ☐ service	I make bread and cookies. I provide a ☐ good ☐ service
I cut and style hair. I provide a ☐ good ☐ service	I grow corn. I provide a ☐ good ☐ service
I help keep the community safe. I provide a ☐ good ☐ service	I clean teeth. I provide a ☐ good ☐ service

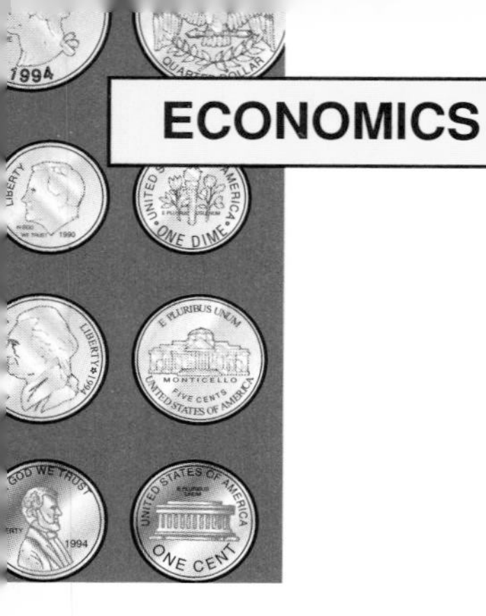

How To Extend The Lesson:

- The yellow pages of telephone books are perfect for reviewing goods and services. Ask a student volunteer to turn to any yellow page of a telephone book and point to an ad or a listing. Read the name of the company (or worker) aloud and give a short description of the work it does. Then have the student state whether the company provides a good or a service (or both). Continue in this same manner until each child has had a turn.

- Divide students into small groups and challenge them to complete the activities below (or similar ones you create).
  —List ten goods that students use.
  —List ten services that students use.
  —List five services that are performed outside.
  —List five services that are performed at a person's home.

- Enlist students to collect business cards (with their parents' help) from various businesses in the community. Place the cards in a center and challenge students to sort the cards into two groups: people who provide goods and people who provide services.

- Have students make an ABC book of goods and services. To do this, list the letters of the alphabet on the chalkboard. As students brainstorm goods and services, write their ideas next to the appropriate letters. Next assign each child one letter and ask her to create a page for an ABC book. To make her page, a student folds a sheet of paper in half and then unfolds it. She writes her letter at the top of the paper; then she labels one half of her paper "Good" and the other half "Service." In the appropriate section, she writes and illustrates a good and a service, each beginning with her letter. Bind the completed projects in alphabetical order between construction-paper covers and title the book "The ABCs Of Goods And Services." Right down to the letter, this book is sure to be a class favorite!

It's Swell To Buy And Sell!

Produce plenty of educated consumers with this lesson!

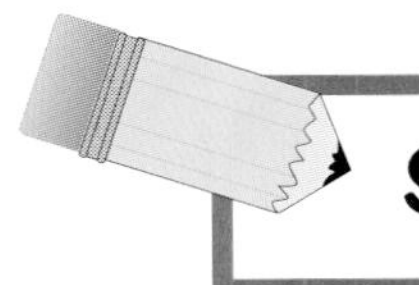

Skill: Identifying producers and consumers

Estimated Lesson Time: 40 minutes

Teacher Preparation:

1. Duplicate page 85 for each student.
2. On the chalkboard, copy the three headings and the list of goods and services shown on the bottom of page 84.

Materials:

1 copy of page 85 per student
crayons

Background Information:
Our economy is comprised of *producers* (sellers) and *consumers* (buyers). People act as consumers when they purchase goods and services. People act as producers when they make products or provide services to sell to others. People can act as both producers and consumers but not at the same time.

Introducing The Lesson:

Tell students that yesterday you walked by a bakery and saw a delicious-looking cookie in the window. Because you were hungry, you went inside and paid the baker a quarter for the cookie. Then explain to students that the baker had something you wanted and you paid him for it. Ask students if they have ever been in a similar situation.

Steps:

1. Tell students that the baker made (or produced) the cookie. He took the role of a *producer.* Then share with students the definition of *producer* from the Background Information on page 83. Next tell students that you took the role of a *consumer* when you purchased the cookie. Share the remainder of the Background Information.

2. Refer students to the list of goods and services on the chalkboard. Read the first item on the list. Ask students to name the producer of the item and possible consumers. Write students' responses in the corresponding columns on the chalkboard.

3. Give each student a copy of page 85. Read the directions aloud; then have each child complete the page independently.

4. Challenge students to complete the Bonus Box activity.

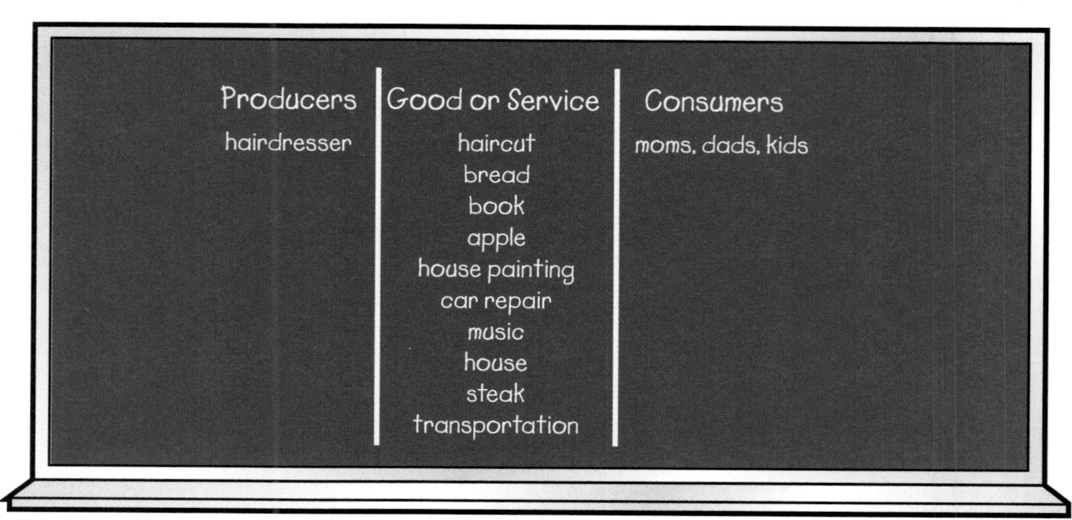

Name ______________________________ Identifying producers and consumers

It's Swell To Buy And Sell!

Look at each picture.
Color the producer in each picture blue.
Color the consumer(s) in each picture red.

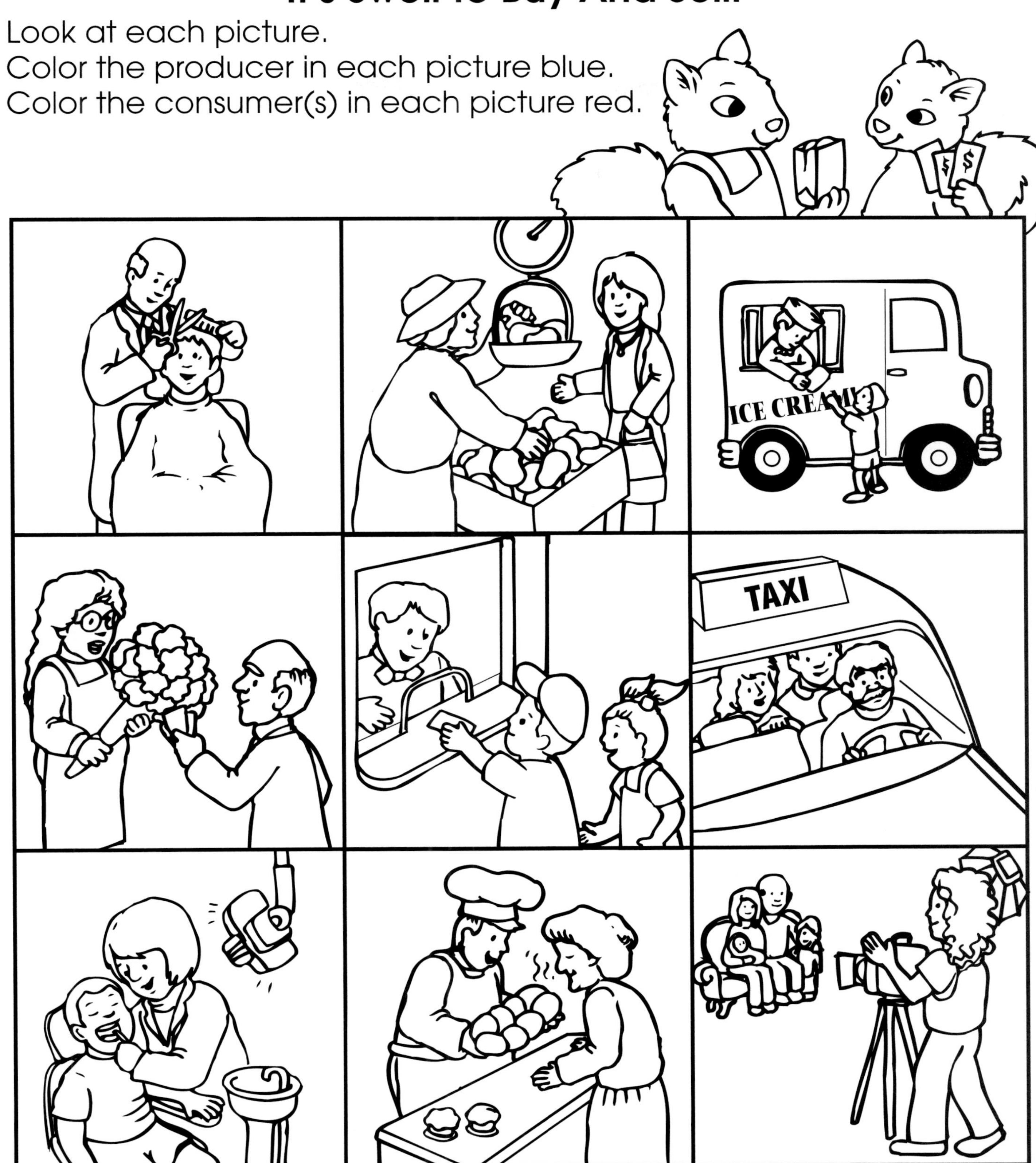

Bonus Box: On the back of this sheet, draw a picture of three things you and your family have purchased this week.

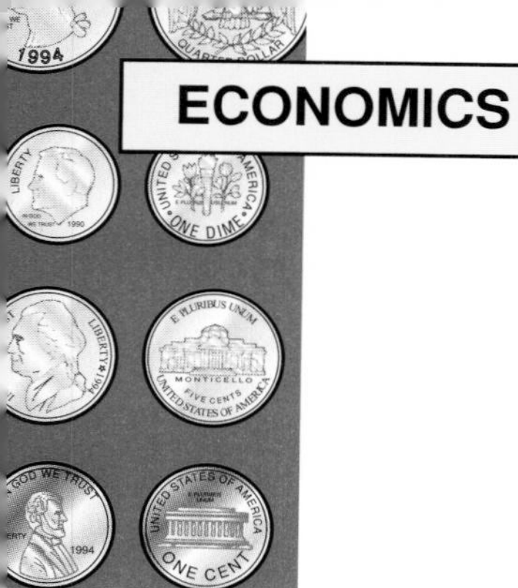

How To Extend The Lesson:

- Students pretend to be producers with this activity. Ask each child to think of a good or a service he would like to provide. Then, on a sheet of drawing paper, have each child create an advertisement for his good or service that would appeal to consumers.

- Challenge students to think of the different situations in which their families are consumers. To do this, each child labels a sheet of colorful construction paper "[Child's name]'s Family Members Are Consumers." Then, from discarded magazines and store circulars, she cuts out pictures or ads of products or services that her family might purchase. Finally, she glues the pictures to the construction paper in a collage fashion.

- Ask your students' parents to act as producers for a class bake sale. Duplicate a class supply of the form shown below. Have each child fill in the date of the bake sale and the date the form needs to be returned and then sign his name. Then have him take the form home to his parents. On the day of the bake sale, set up a toy cash register and price the baked goods. Also give each student enough play money to purchase one baked good and juice. Then invite students to make desired purchases from the classroom bakery. What a tasty way for students to act as consumers!

Dear Parent,

We have been learning about producers and consumers. We would like to have a bake sale on ________________________ to practice being consumers. But we need some producers! If you would like to help, please fill out the bottom of this form and return it to school by ________________.

Thank you!

____

If you can participate, please check one (or more!) of the following:

_______ I'd like to bake cookies.
_______ I'd like to bake cupcakes.
_______ I'd like to provide juice.
_______ I'd like to help out at the "bakery."

Spending Money

Cash in on this profitable lesson, which helps youngsters identify many different uses of money.

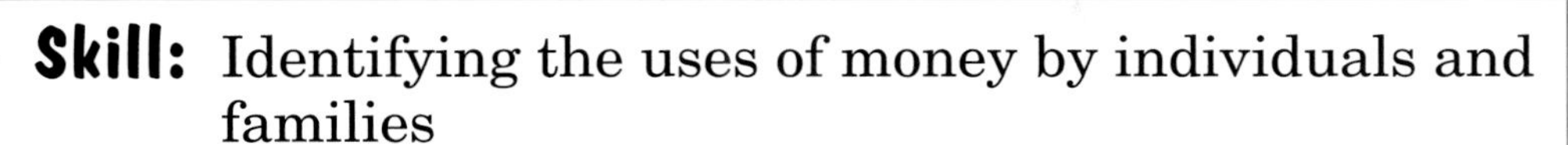

Skill: Identifying the uses of money by individuals and families

Estimated Lesson Time: 35 minutes

Teacher Preparation:

1. Duplicate page 89 for each student.
2. Draw and label a house, a television, a burger, and a pair of pants near each other on the chalkboard. On another area of the chalkboard, draw a person jogging and a person walking his dog.

Materials:

1 copy of page 89 per student

Background Information:

Most families spend the majority of their *income,* or money they earn for the jobs they do, on basic necessities like food, shelter, and clothing. But families also spend money on wants like entertainment, toys, and travel.

Introducing The Lesson:

Refer students to the drawings on the chalkboard. Challenge the students to determine how the items are grouped. Lead students to see that the items are sorted into two categories: things that cost money and things that do not cost money.

Steps:

1. Use the Background Information on page 87 as you explain to students that money can be used in a variety of ways.

2. Invite each child in turn to share with the class something that either he or his family uses money to purchase. Record students' responses on the chalkboard. Make two sections: Family Purchases and Individual Purchases.

3. Give each student a copy of page 89. Read the directions aloud; then have each child complete the reproducible, using the student-generated list for assistance as necessary.

Name ____ *Identifying the uses of money*

Spending Money

What does your family use money to buy?
What do you use money to buy?
Write the items on the bills.

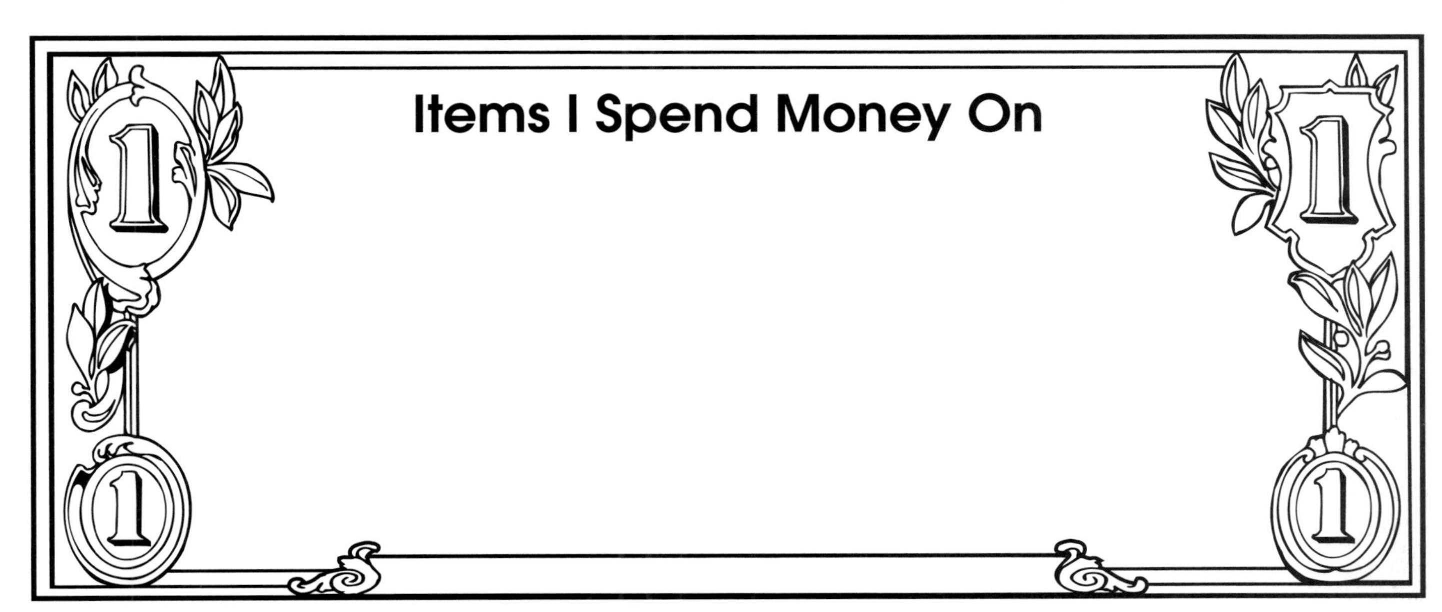

What is the most important item your family spends money on?
Why do you think so?

____

____

____

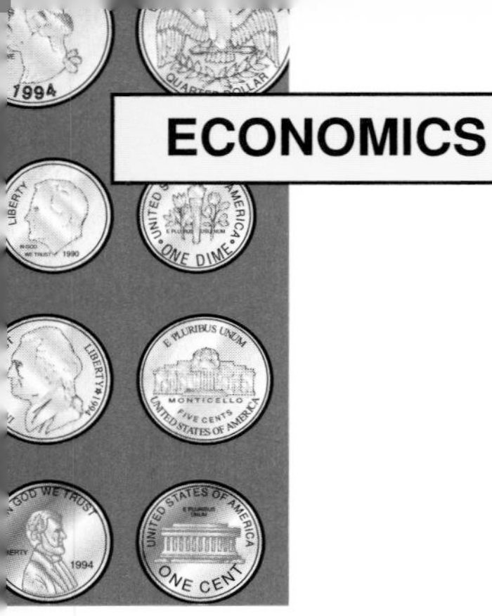

How To Extend The Lesson:

- Just exactly what do families spend money on in a single day? Challenge students to find out. Have each child record on a sheet of paper the items on which his family spends money during one day. After each child has returned his paper, enlist students' help in making a graph to show which kinds of items were the most frequently purchased.

- Read aloud the story *Alexander, Who Used To Be Rich Last Sunday* by Judith Viorst (Aladdin Paperbacks, 1980). Afterward challenge students to list all the items on which Alexander spent money. Write students' responses on the chalkboard. Then, during a second oral reading, check off each item on the list that students remembered correctly and add any items they left off. Next lead students in a discussion about wise uses of money. Then ask student volunteers to share times they wished they had spent their money a bit more wisely!

- This class book reinforces the idea that not everything in life costs money. On a sheet of drawing paper, have each child draw a picture of an activity that her family could participate in that doesn't cost any money. After each child has shared her work, bind the papers between two construction-paper covers and add the title "Some Of The Best Things In Life Are Free."

Collecting seashells at the beach

A Job For Everyone

If you're antsy for your youngsters to learn the benefits of cooperation, then try this division-of-labor activity.

Skill: Participating in a division-of-labor activity

Estimated Lesson Time: 30 minutes

Teacher Preparation:

1. Duplicate page 93 for each student plus one extra.
2. Write on the chalkboard the following jobs and their corresponding numbers.
   - Student 1: Cut on the bold lines and fold on the thin lines.
   - Student 2: Color the ant.
   - Student 3: Trace the "Thank You!" using different-colored crayons.
   - Student 4: Copy [teacher's name] on the line.

Materials:

1 copy of page 93 per student plus one extra
crayons
scissors

Background Information:

Division of labor is the dividing of work so that each person has a specific job to do. It produces more and better services for the same amount of work. Each person can specialize in just her task and therefore do her task better and more quickly. With a division of labor, no one has to do all of the work.

Introducing The Lesson:

Ask your youngsters to think about the people who work in their school cafeteria. Then have students name the different jobs that are done in the cafeteria. Examples might include grocery shopping or ordering from vendors, cooking the food, serving the food, or working as a cashier. Ask students why they think more than one person works in the cafeteria. Guide students to see that a group effort is necessary for the large task of cooking lunch for the entire school.

Steps:

1. Explain to students that sometimes a big job is divided into several smaller jobs. Then the smaller jobs are given to different workers. The workers learn to do their jobs well because they are only working on one task. Therefore, the work can be done more quickly. Share the Background Information on page 93.

2. Ask students to think about the many deeds that parent helpers and the members of the PTA do for the children. Then tell students that they will use division of labor to make thank-you cards for these special helpers.

3. Divide the class into groups of four and assign each child a number from 1 to 4. Refer students to the list of jobs on the chalkboard. As you read aloud each job, demonstrate how to complete it using a copy of page 93.

4. Distribute a copy of page 93 to each child. Explain that each child will complete only the task that corresponds to his number and then pass the project to the next person in the group. Emphasize that the goal of the activity is not to finish first, but for each group member to do his job the best he can.

5. Provide time for each group to complete four thank-you cards. Then have students discuss the advantages of working together. Enlist students' help in presenting the cards to volunteers who help at your school.

Use with Steps 3, 4, and 5 on page 92.

Thank you
for being so kind.

You are a wonderful volunteer!

From ______________________'s class

- Have students create a favorite snacktime treat, Ants-On-A-Log, by dividing up the work. To begin, divide students into groups of three and assign each group member a different job: wash and cut celery, spread the peanut butter, or place the raisins on the log. Provide each group with paper towels, access to water, three napkins, two plastic knives, celery stalk(s), peanut butter, and raisins. Then have each group work together, division of labor–style, to create three tasty snacks!

- Share *The Little Red Hen* by Paul Galdone (Houghton Mifflin Company, 1985) with your youngsters. Discuss how the story might have been different if each animal had shared in the work. Then, during a second oral reading, have students respond with "I will" rather than "Not I" each time the little red hen asks the lazy animals to do some work. Conclude your oral reading by changing the ending of the story so the animal friends enjoy the rewards of their work together.

- Explain to students that most of the work done in an ant colony is done by the worker ants. Some jobs available to worker ants include: nurse (cares for eggs and larvae), construction worker (digs new rooms and tunnels and carries dirt outside), hunter (goes in search of food and brings it back to the nest), and security guard (defends the nest against enemies). After sharing this information, ask your youngsters to create jobs for your classroom colony. List the job titles and descriptions on a chart. Then have each child personalize and cut out a construction-paper copy of the ant pattern shown. Laminate the ants and the chart. To use the resulting job helper board, tape an ant cutout beside each job description. Each week assign new jobs using an established method of rotation.

Answer Keys

Page 17

School rules:

- Listen to your teacher.
- Be on time.
- Raise your hand.
- Walk in the hallway.
- Stand for the pledge.

Home rules:

- Clean your room.
- Make your bed.
- Go to bed on time.
- Brush your teeth.
- Listen to your parents.

Page 25

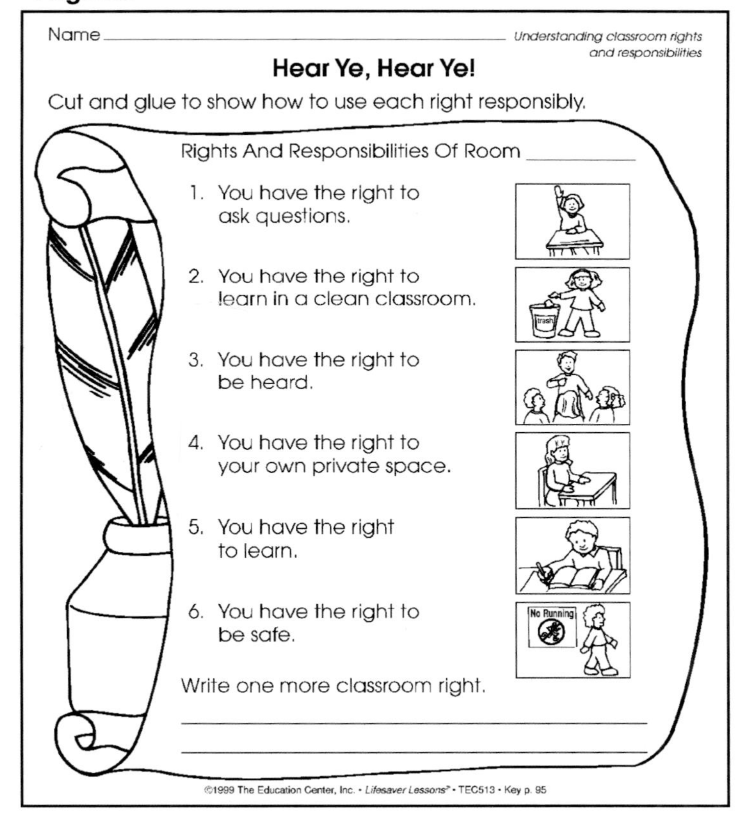

Name ____________ *Understanding classroom rights and responsibilities*

Hear Ye, Hear Ye!

Cut and glue to show how to use each right responsibly.

Rights And Responsibilities Of Room ________

1. You have the right to ask questions.
2. You have the right to learn in a clean classroom.
3. You have the right to be heard.
4. You have the right to your own private space.
5. You have the right to learn.
6. You have the right to be safe.

Write one more classroom right.

©1999 The Education Center, Inc. • *Lifesaver Lessons*® • TEC513 • Key p. 95

Page 65

Schools Of The Past: slate, one-room school, log bench, tin lunch pail, recitation, dunce cap

Schools Of Today: lunch bag, school bus, computer, notebook, school, desk and chair

Page 81

Mini Book
Use with Steps 3 and 4 on page 80.

My Goods And Services Mini Book

by ____________ Name

teacher — I help children learn. I provide a ☐ good ☑ service

seamstress — I make clothes. I provide a ☑ good ☐ service

baker — I make bread and cookies. I provide a ☑ good ☐ service

hairdresser — I cut and style hair. I provide a ☐ good ☑ service

farmer — I grow corn. I provide a ☑ good ☐ service

police officer — I help keep the community safe. I provide a ☐ good ☑ service

dentist — I clean teeth. I provide a ☐ good ☑ service

©1999 The Education Center, Inc. • *Lifesaver Lessons*® • TEC513 • Key p. 95

Grade 1 Social Studies Management Checklist

SKILLS	PAGES	DATE(S) USED	COMMENTS
ME & MY COMMUNITY			
Self-Esteem	3		
Different Family Structures	7		
Community Helpers	11		
GOVERNMENT & CITIZENSHIP			
Rules At Home And School	15		
Classroom Citizenship	19		
Classroom Rights And Responsibilities	23		
Democratic Decision Making	27		
United States Symbols	31		
MAP SKILLS			
Map Symbols And Map Keys	35		
Creating A Classroom Map	39		
Cardinal Directions	43		
OUR NEIGHBORS			
Holidays Around The World	47		
Families Around The World	51		
Homes Around The World	55		
HISTORY			
Sequencing Holidays On A Timeline	59		
Schools Of Today And The Past	63		
Significant Historical Figures	67		
ECONOMICS			
Needs And Wants	71		
Shortages	75		
Goods And Services	79		
Producers And Consumers	83		
Money As A Means Of Exchange	87		
Division Of Labor	91		